D0879321

# Contextualizing Theological Education

**Theodore Brelsford** and
**P. Alice Rogers,** *editors*

THE
PILGRIM
PRESS
Cleveland

The Pilgrim Press
700 Prospect Avenue
Cleveland, Ohio 44115-1100
thepilgrimpress.com

♲ Printed in the United States of America on acid-free paper that contains
   post-consumer fiber.


12  11  10  09  08    5  4  3  2


**Library of Congress Cataloging-in-Publication Data**

Contextualizing theological education / Theodore Brelsford and P. Alice Rogers,
   editors.
        p.   cm.
    ISBN 978-0-8298-1784-3 (alk. paper)
    1. Theology – Study and teaching.  2. Christianity and culture.  I. Brelsford,
Theodore.  II. Rogers, P. Alice, 1961-
    BV4022.C66 2008
    230.071′1 – dc22                                        2007045280

# Contents

# Foreword

This book must be read in context. It's the culmination of a long conversation over nearly four decades, in a southern Methodist seminary, among theologians trained in a variety of disciplines, searching together for the best way to prepare students for ministry. This book's context is historical, denominational, institutional, and intellectual. It is also composed of gender, ethnic, race, and class perspectives as well as insights gleaned from age and classroom experience. Its context is personal, vocational, cultural, and communal. At the same time its context is local, yet global; particular, yet universal; and diverse, yet common. Identity and place are also its context. By complexifying what we mean by context, *Contextualizing Theological Education* has moved us well beyond Barth's pastor who holds a Bible in one hand and the newspaper in the other.

Thanks to the Candler School of Theology's faculty at Emory University in Atlanta, theological educators have a chance to learn about what happens to a faculty, a curriculum, and ministry students when contextual education becomes the heart and pulse of theological education. From the early days of the Supervised Ministry program to today's Contextual Education curriculum, Candler has developed one of the most effective models of teaching and learning ministry in context.

For too long theological education has faced several persistent challenges: Is the academy beholden to the guilds and not sufficiently attentive to the church and its ministry? Has the seminary turned away from the congregation to such an extent as to be irrelevant? Do field education and "practical" courses bear the weight (and criticism) of training students to be competent ministers? The Candler faculty wisely found a way to answer "no" to these questions. Contextual education is designed to move faculty closer to the everyday realities of ministry, by immersing groups of students with a faculty member in parish and social ministry contexts for a year, and by allowing the contexts of ministry to become a classroom for all. Faculty have not sacrificed the academy's intellectual rigor or standards by moving into context, but have found that examining real situations makes the theological disciplines more relevant and vital to students. In prison visits, congregational meetings, educational events, and advocacy work, the church's theological reflection on creation, sin and grace, suffering, the cross and resurrection, and its embodied practices, rituals, and norms all become vital sources for understanding and interpreting God's presence in our lives. Context is incarnational.

The authors of this book do not make contextual education sound easy — it is labor intensive and demanding. In addition to sharing pedagogical shortcomings, they give us a glimpse into the wonder of contextual teaching and learning. One of their most daring moves was to demand that all faculty teach a contextual education course, recognizing that not all have the gifts for such teaching, but that such a requirement was necessary to engage the curriculum as a context. To teach and learn contextually demands a price. Both faculty and students are challenged to integrate their sense of vocation, theological knowledge, and ministry competence in the light of the messy realities of lived faith.

Contextual education is not a passing fad. We all teach in a context, about contexts, and toward context. By attending to the variety and diversity of the everyday as a mystery rather than a problem to be solved or classified, contextual education fosters better practice in ministry. It is not, finally, the goal or purpose of seminary education. Rather, contextual education is a creative pedagogical strategy and theological commitment designed to cultivate habits of mind and spiritual dispositions in ministers who can lead passionately and effectively. Candler's bet has been that this kind of teaching and learning is the surest path to that goal. I think it's a bet many theological educators will find worth taking.

*Kathleen A. Cahalan*
*Collegeville, Minnesota*

# Acknowledgments

We are grateful to the past and present faculty members and administrators of Candler School of Theology for their vision, commitment, and dedication to contextualizing the curriculum for the purpose of educating faithful and creative leaders for the church's ministries in the world. This effort has been marked by numerous faculty conversations, by the commitment of each faculty member to lead Contextual Education Reflection Groups, and by individual faculty members intentionally developing and redesigning courses to advance this endeavor. We especially thank the faculty members who have shared their experiences of this process in the essays written for this volume.

We are also deeply grateful to Lilly Endowment Inc. for their generous support and partnership in envisioning, implementing, and re-visioning vibrant programmatic structures for connecting theological education more closely to the contextual realities and needs of the church.

# Contributors

**Claire Bischoff** is a doctoral student in the Graduate Division of Religion, Emory University, and co-editor of *My Red Couch and Other Stories on Seeking a Feminist Faith.*

**Elizabeth M. Bounds,** Associate Professor of Christian Ethics at Candler School of Theology and Director of the Graduate Division of Religion, Emory University, is author of *Coming Together/Coming Apart: Religion, Community, and Modernity.*

**Theodore Brelsford,** Assistant Professor of Religion and Education and Director of the Religious Education Program at Candler School of Theology, Emory University, is co-author of *We Are the Church Together: Cultural Diversity and Congregational Life.*

**W. Harrison Daniel,** Assistant Professor of the Practice of History and Mission at Candler School of Theology, Emory University, is author of *Practicing the Future Perfect: Ministry Practices and Communal Mission in the New Testament,* and *Historical Atlas of World Methodism and Related Movements.*

**Noel Leo Erskine,** Associate Professor of Theology and Ethics at Candler School of Theology, Emory University, is author of *From Garvey to Marley: Rastafari Theology.*

**David Jenkins,** Lecturer in Church and Community Ministries and Co-director of Contextual Education at Candler School of Theology, Emory University, is the author of *Hospitality: Risking Welcome.*

**Luke Timothy Johnson,** Robert W. Woodruff Professor of New Testament and Christian Origins at Candler School of Theology, Emory University, is author of *The Creed: What Christians Believe and Why it Matters* and many other books.

**Joy Ann McDougall,** Associate Professor of Systematic Theology at Candler School of Theology, Emory University, has written *The Pilgrimage of Love: Moltmann on the Trinity and the Christian Life,* as well as articles on gender and vocation in theological education.

**Mary Elizabeth Mullino Moore,** Professor of Religion and Education and Director of the Program for Women in Theology and Ministry at Candler School of Theology, Emory University, is author of *Teaching as a Sacramental Act* and numerous other books, and co-editor of *Practical Theology and Hermeneutics.*

**P. Alice Rogers** is Lecturer in Practical Theology, Co-director of Contextual Education, and Director of the Teaching Parish Program at Candler School of Theology, Emory University.

**John Senior,** a doctoral student in the Graduate Division of Religion at Emory University, has served as Research Fellow for the Contextual Education Program at Candler School of Theology. He studies political theology and democratic practices.

**Brent A. Strawn,** Associate Professor of Old Testament at Candler School of Theology, Emory University, has authored *What Is Stronger Than a Lion? Leonine Image and Metaphor in the Hebrew Bible and the Ancient Near East,* and is co-editor of *Qumran Studies: New Approaches, New Questions.*

**M. Thomas Thangaraj,** D. W. & Ruth Brooks Associate Professor of World Christianity at the Candler School of Theology, Emory University, has written *The Crucified Guru: An Experiment in Cross-Cultural Theology* and other books.

**Robert W. Winstead** is the Senior Pastor at Haygood Memorial United Methodist Church in Atlanta, as well as a Teaching Supervisor for the Teaching Parish Program and Adjunct Instructor in Leadership and Administration at Candler School of Theology, Emory University.

# Introduction

## Theodore Brelsford

Graduate professional theological education as formally carried out in modern Western culture has three primary contexts and three primary constituencies to whom it must be responsible: academy, church, and society. To contextualize theological education, as we describe in this volume, is to engage in theological education with a conscious intent to integrate these three contexts; to locate learning in all three contexts; and to hold teaching, learning, and knowledge in each of these contexts accountable to the others. Such integration of learning and interrelating of contexts is increasingly important and increasingly difficult.

One reason for the increasing difficulty of this integration is a weakening of the formative power of both church and academy. Whereas once upon a time most students came to seminary reasonably well formed in the traditions of the church, and reasonably well formed in the liberal arts traditions of the academy, they now often come loosely formed in the church (if at all), and with a utilitarian view of education as means to some professional end rather than as liberative engagement in the human arts and sciences. Students cannot readily integrate learning in ecclesial and academic traditions in which they are not yet well formed.

One reason for the increasing importance of contextual integration is a growing perception in the culture at large of both the academy and the church as marginal or irrelevant to the practical concerns of life in the "real world." If we intend seminary education to matter and make a difference in society, church, and the world, then what we do in seminary must be integrally related with significant social and global realities. The authors of the present volume believe that thoroughgoing contextualization of theological education is fundamentally important for vital and vibrant theological education in the twenty-first century. Such contextualization not only enriches theological education but also has much to contribute to the church and larger world. Indeed, seminaries are well positioned to make precisely this kind of integrative contribution.

As William M. Sullivan puts it in his introduction to *Educating Clergy*, "professional schools are hybrid institutions."[1] They are part of the academic tradition of rationality, part of the world of practices of a particular profession, and are partly identified with and governed by the normative knowledge of the profession. Sullivan terms these the "three internships" of professional education (and three domains of professional formation): cognitive, practical, and normative. Drawing on this notion of three internships, we suggest that "contextual" education seeks to connect the cognitive and the normative via the practical; or, the academic and professional "apprenticeships" via practices. As such, contextual education seeks to model and promote a particular, integrated way of being in the world.

While seminaries are part of the broader landscape of professional education (along with law, medicine, education, and others), they also have a distinctive theological orientation and mission. Seminaries seek to prepare persons for spiritual leadership in church and society and for modeling the living of responsible and integrated lives before God. As such, seminaries themselves bear major responsibility for embodying and modeling contextual integration. This is a significant burden. The essays in this volume explore a range of meanings, challenges, and opportunities of contextual integration in theological education as well as provide specific pedagogical strategies and insights out of our own experiences as theological educators. All contributors have played some role in the Contextual Education Program at Emory University's Candler School of Theology; many also have teaching and pastoral experience in other institutions.

---

1. Charles R. Foster et al., *Educating Clergy: Teaching Practices and the Pastoral Imagination*, 5.

## *Contextualization at Candler as a Case Study*

Beginning in 1969, similar to many other Protestant seminaries at the time, Emory University's Candler School of Theology initiated a supervised ministry program aimed at contextualizing theological learning in relation to the church and various social or clinical settings. Students served in part-time internship-like positions in these settings under the direction of a site supervisor and met weekly in small groups on campus with a faculty member and supervisor to reflect on their experiences in the ministry sites. This program involved the entire faculty in such small group teaching and contextual reflection, and served as an integral part of the M.Div. curriculum for nearly three decades.

In 1998, Candler launched a comprehensive new program in contextual education intentionally designed to alter the future shape of its curriculum.[2] Candler had long been committed to educating its students in direct relationship to ministry contexts. But the shift to "contextualized education" for ministry marked a new era in theological education at Candler and reflects a similar shift in theological education more broadly.

While the supervised ministry program was explicitly modeled on Clinical Pastoral Education — with its psychological and confrontational orientation — contextual education was to be more explicitly theological and ecclesiological. When the supervised ministry program was launched in 1969, students tended to be predominantly male, white, young, Methodist, and well formed in the faith traditions of the church. The reality of an increasingly diverse student body, of which fewer and fewer are well formed in the church, made clear the need for a formative emphasis on the connectedness and coherence of theological reflection and practice rather than confrontational small group dynamics as a primary methodology in the formation of future leaders for the church. The new Contextual Education Program aimed at embodying such connectedness and coherence between and among church, academy, and society and sought to draw the entire faculty together around this mission.

---

2. This initiative was supported by and continues to benefit from generous funding from Lilly Endowment Inc.

The core of Candler's Contextual Education Program since 1998 has consisted of M.Div. students working four hours a week in a social service ministry or clinical site during their first year, and five hours a week in an ecclesial site during their second year. In each year students are divided into diverse groups of ten to twelve and meet weekly in a two-hour reflection group co-taught by a faculty member and an active ministry professional. In the first year these reflection groups consist of students all serving at the same placement site, and the supervisor from that site co-teaches the reflection group. The first year social and clinical settings include a range of sites such as hospitals, retirement/assisted living facilities, prisons, homeless shelters, a children's home, etc.

In the second year of Contextual Education the program focuses on ecclesial practices within congregational settings. Students covenant to work five hours a week in a church or campus ministry setting relevant to their denominational affiliation and/or vocational goals under the supervision of an ordained site supervisor. Whatever the setting, all students experience ministry in at least five areas: preaching and worship, administration, education, mission and outreach, and congregational/pastoral care.

United Methodist students serving under Episcopal appointment fulfill the contextual education requirement through participation in Teaching Parish reflection groups led by ordained elders in the United Methodist Church. Students are grouped geographically and meet off campus at a church central to their geographic location.

The Candler faculty initially held hopes that this Contextual Education Program would provide for, or at least plant seeds for, the integration of theological learning and practice throughout the curriculum; now, almost ten years later, those hopes are being realized. The contextualization initiative has involved the entire faculty in teaching the Contextual Education Reflection Seminars together with local ministry supervisors, has led to the contextualization and redesign of individual courses by 20 percent of the faculty across the curriculum, and has informed a recent thoroughgoing revision of the entire curriculum, including the incorporation of first-year contextual experiences into introductory Arts of Ministry courses.

Thus, at the time of this writing Candler is in the later phases of a decade's worth of rather rapid and dramatic development in the way we do theological education. In view of both our core Contextual Education Program with its site placements and reflection seminars, and our larger efforts at contextualization in courses across our curriculum, this volume provides some perspective on changes currently under way by reflecting on some historical and theoretical aspects of contextual education, drawing pedagogical lessons from our teaching, and naming challenges and opportunities for the future.

## Historical Background of Contextualization in Theological Education in the United States

This shift in the way that theological education is understood and undertaken at Candler is part of a larger groundswell change in theological education across North America. A generation ago the issue of tensions between academic and ecclesial orientations in theological education was a notable concern, with the debates primarily orienting around concerns for theoretical grounding or methodological authority.[3] Part of the current shift under way is connected to a serious wavering of faith in the primacy of theory and the possibility of grounding. There is instead now excitement and hope around a new focus on formation in practices rooted in traditions and manifest in dynamic contemporary contexts.

Reporting on the beginning phases of Candler's Contextual Education Program in a 2000 article in the *Christian Century*, Luke T. Johnson and Charlotte McDaniel noted that contextual education entails three primary assumptions. The first assumption is that "theology involves responding to the living God in diverse human situations" and the dynamic realities of actual ever-changing contexts. Thus it is that "contextual education" has become a focus of our attention and a way of naming a central concern at Candler and other theological educational institutions.

A second primary assumption is that "theology involves specific practices as much as it does religious concepts and experiences." The

---

3. See Edward Farley, *The Fragility of Knowledge: Theological Education in the Church and University.*

conviction here is that what is actually done is what actually matters, and that ideas and theories actually grow out of practices more dependably than vice versa. The practices of ministry have always been a vital part of theological education. Those practices are increasingly seen as constitutive of rather than derivative from theological convictions.

Finally, a third assumption is that "theological education requires attention to personal formation and not simply learning of specialized lore and skills." This, again, is not new to theological education, but this renewed interest in (if not yet fully shared commitment to) personal formation points to a significant shift in the "location" and self-understanding of theological education.

From its inception, of course, clergy education in the United States has been concerned with preparation and formation of persons for ministry in specific local church contexts. In that sense theological education has always been connected to and shaped by ministry contexts. Indeed, prior to the nineteenth century an extended residency internship in a parish following an academic course in divinity was considered an essential and expected part of preparation for ministry. Thus, theological education was located explicitly both in the academy and in the church.[4]

However, during the nineteenth century, theological education gradually moved out of the regular college curriculum and into professional schools or freestanding denominational seminaries, paralleling the advent of professional schools of medicine and law, and the crystallization of distinctive fields of scientific enquiry across the university. Now rather than "reading theology" in college and then apprenticing with a master pastor, a more integrated and complete professional education for ministry was deemed possible within the seminary. Thus, rather ironically, since the nineteenth-century migration of theological education out of the regular college curriculum, formal clergy education in the United States has been conducted largely in and through academic institutions rather than through apprenticeship in churches, and in and through modern academic

---

4. For a discussion of the early history of American theological education see Clark Gilpin, *A Preface to Theology.*

disciplines intentionally grounded in presumed universalizable theories rather than presumed contextually specific ministry practices. The primary model and context for theological education in the modern West has been and continues to be "the academy."

The relative integrity of the ways academic theological education currently connects to professional ministry practice is seen differently by different constituencies. The recent Carnegie Foundation study of education across the professions finds that attention to professional formation in theological education has been and continues to be far more intentional and integrated than in other professions such as law, medicine, and engineering. At the same time there is a prevalent perception in many churches and among growing numbers of theological educators of a problematic gap between theological education and contexts of ministry. Efforts at contextualizing theological education aim at narrowing this gap via teaching practices that nurture integration of cognitive, practical, and normative learning.

## *Current Critiques and Trends*

Current contextual theological education efforts assume a closer connection between ministry and seminary classroom contexts, and a more equitable role for contexts beyond the classroom in the overall project of theological education. From the beginning, as already noted, internships or apprenticeships or field placement experiences have had a place in graduate theological education. But for most of the past century, from the perspective of the academy, these have been largely seen as opportunities for the application and testing out of theories, or at best as an opportunity for a different kind of on-the-job learning. The recent shift of attention to the significance of contextual learning beyond the classroom has heightened awareness of the significance of the context of the classroom and the academy. The seminary classroom, as it turns out, is a very particular (and some might say peculiar) context, which shapes learning in very particular ways. As Sullivan puts it, "Like many other professional schools, seminaries heavily emphasize learning that takes place in the classroom. Because students typically study at some remove from the actual practice of clergy life, much of the teaching and learning in seminaries has an unmistakable academic cast that emphasizes cognitive mastery of concepts and knowledge."[5]

"Contextual education" attempts to broaden learning beyond the cognitive and to make intentional and intelligent use of specific contexts as sites of learning and as teaching and learning experiences in and of themselves. Middle-class U.S. American students carrying cinder blocks, for example, to help build a community center in Honduras is a valuable contextual learning experience. But so also is a university theology school lecture on Old Testament erotic poetry and contemporary pop-culture pornography; and European American students' revelatory recognition of their own cultural heritage when being confronted with stories of their Asian, Asian American, Hispanic, and African American peers' particular cultural formation; and other students' classroom encounter with a barrage of artistic Asian, African, Native American, and other images of Christ.

These examples (drawn from the chapters that follow) of contextual learning in theological education illumine one more characteristic assumption of contextual education: theology is and ought to be public and political. This implies attentiveness and responsibility to the social contexts of theological education. Efforts to contextualize theological education are driven by the conviction that theological education should be aimed at and in the service of ministry that makes a real material difference in the real material world. Each of the essays in this volume focuses in varying ways on making pedagogical use of the dynamic relationships between and among social, ecclesial, and academic contexts in order to strengthen students' abilities to skillfully use academic theological tools to make real differences in the real world. In this sense the theological classroom becomes a training ground or a practice space for life and ministry in the public arena. We offer this volume as a contribution to the ongoing effort to understand and strengthen this theological educational mission. Assuming that thoroughgoing contextualization of theological education is fundamentally important for vital and vibrant theological education in the twenty-first century, the questions we address in what follows have to do with what this means and how we do it.

---

5. Foster et al., *Educating Clergy*, 7.

## *Overview of the Book*

In an effort to further define and advance the work of contextualization of theological education this volume provides theoretical reflections, practical insights, and critical discussions from our own work in contextual education. Some central questions we address include: What are some of the primary relevant meanings of "contextualization," and what are historical roots of contextualization in relation to theology and theological education? What does it mean to reflect theologically or think theologically in relation to particular contexts, and how do we help persons learn to do so well? How does heightened awareness of context contribute to theological reflection and theological learning? How do certain social and cultural contexts shape theological learning and how may these be used as pedagogical resources to strengthen and advance contextual learning? And what does all of this look like in particular courses and particular academic disciplines?

We write, as we must, with reference to our particular institutional contexts, academic disciplines, courses we have taught, and our own life experiences. But we do so in order to engage ourselves and our readers in contextual learning. The point of contextual education and contextual learning is not that all of our experiences are context bound, such that experiences in one context cannot be relevant for another context. Rather, the point is to become well practiced at gleaning knowledge, wisdom, and understanding from contextual experiences — which knowledge, wisdom, and understanding is indeed portable to future experiences in varying contexts — while also remaining aware that wisdom gleaned from past contextual experiences *may not* necessarily be adequate in all future contexts. Learning is by definition portable. Even if not fully adequate, it is portable from one context to another and from one person to another, or else we do not say that a thing has been learned.

We engage here in contextual theological reflection in order to identify contextually grounded lessons, insights, and questions we now carry with us and believe useful. We have been energized and educated in our sharing of these lessons, insights, and questions with each other. We hope that readers may similarly benefit.

Part One provides theological, philosophical, and historical perspectives on meanings and implications of "context and contextualization in theological education." At the outset Elizabeth Bounds takes up the task of defining theological reflection, discussing a few central problems inherent in it and suggesting ways to better teach it. As Bounds lays out, theological reflection essentially involves "integrated analysis" of one's self, one's theology, and one's specific situation. As such theological reflection is a central and basic concern of theological education. Bounds provides images of non-integration in the form of scenes from actual Contextual Education Reflection Seminars she has taught in order to name and clarify the pedagogical challenges of theological reflection as integration. The chapter also names curricular challenges and makes specific suggestions for creating learning experiences that enable students to practice integration of personal experience with cognitive understandings of theological traditions and analysis of particular social and ecclesial contexts.

The term and the concept of "contextualization" in relation to theology and theological education were born in the work of the World Council of Churches. W. Harrison Daniel traces the development of contextualization initiatives in the global church beginning with a Taiwanese theological educator named Shoki Coe, which were taken up by the WCC's Theological Education Fund. Coe named "context" (along with eschatology or time, and catholicity or space) as one of three basic categories of theological discourse that should inform effective training for pastoral leadership and the transmission of faith. Daniel illumines this historical development as an indigenous response to imperialistic tendencies in Western missionary initiatives and helps us see ways that the historical roots of theological contextualization continue to underlie and inform our current efforts.

Given this historical background and building on the notion of theological reflection as integrated analysis, John Senior and I examine some philosophical and pedagogical meanings, functions, and dynamics of contextual theological thinking. This chapter proposes a way of conceiving theological thinking as "catching theology in action" and "reconstructing theology in practice." A primary concern taken up in the chapter is that of understanding and nurturing skillful contextual theological reflection in the context of seminary or divinity/theology school courses. The chapter suggests ways of understanding theological thinking as a dimension of contextual education that entails processes of bringing out what is inside of students so that this may be critically reconstructed in the learning community and then reintegrated by students such that their ways of thinking and being are changed. In so doing, we seek to describe a model for skillful theological thinking and a means for creating possibilities for reconstructing functional theology in practice.

One highly effective way of bringing real, functional theology into the classroom is by tapping the resources of students' experiences, especially experiences students have already had in contexts of ministry. P. Alice Rogers and Robert Winstead explore ways of drawing on experiences of students serving in ecclesial contexts as pedagogical resources for contextualizing classroom learning. As the authors point out, many seminaries enroll significant numbers of students already serving churches at least part time. This division of time and attention between church and academy can become a source of distraction and frustration for both students and faculty members. This chapter focuses instead on ways seminary teachers can use students' ecclesial experience to enrich and relevantly contextualize learning for all students — those serving churches as well as those not currently doing so.

The practice of Christian faith, of course, extends well beyond what happens in church and in one's personal piety. In the final chapter of this section, Noel Erskine reminds us that theological education must do more than ask about the continuities between church and classroom; it must also seek for continuities and explore relationships between the oppressed in our societies and the classrooms in which theological education occurs. Erskine mines the historical developments of black theology (and especially its stubbornly open posture toward white theology together with its stubborn ignorance of black women) for clues and resources for developing excellence in contextually responsible theological teaching. The fact that black male theologians were able to unwittingly ignore and render invisible their own sisters and mothers, while at the same time working so hard to resist white patterns of exclusion and oppression, illustrates poignantly how very easy it is to engage theology in ways that completely ignore vital dimensions of even our most immediate contexts and leave a painful gap between our theory and our practice. Ultimately Erskine wishes to address the question of what it actually means to include "others" in the classroom and advocates a pedagogy that is an invitation to love God.

Part Two provides critical insights into "contextualizing the curriculum." Many of us first gain awareness of the significance and particularity of our own native contexts by exposure to or even immersion in a "foreign" context. David O. Jenkins examines ways that notable changes in context create possibilities of transformative learning. Recollections of a ten-day "experiential" in Honduras as part of a semester-long course provide a focal point for these reflections. Such changes of context often transform teacher-student relationships as well as conceptions of relationships between "developed" and "developing" countries, and between theological concepts and life experiences. In these situations students learn skills for communication and connection across cultural differences and with persons unlike themselves. Stories of students' international and cross-cultural experiences in Honduras and Mexico shared here make this clear and expose some of these dynamics. But as some of the students who made these trips observe, similar dynamics and opportunities are also present in one's own city and one's own neighborhood, and even within academic classrooms, as students begin to more fully recognize and appreciate diversity and contextual realities all around them.

One of the theologians on our faculty most keenly attuned to contextual concerns embodies contemporary realities of cross-cultural, global experience. M. Thomas Thangaraj began his ministry in the church and theological education in his native India. In his chapter in this volume Thangaraj explains that his commitment to contextualized theology began as a commitment to articulate and preserve the rich heritage of uniquely Indian Christian theology. Over the past two decades at Candler, Professor Thangaraj has worked to assist the growth of global consciousness among students and especially to help them recognize the varying, contextually specific forms that Christianity takes around the world. Thangaraj argues that contextuality or contextual awareness is the natural outcome of combining local and global awareness. Through descriptions of a course on "Images of Christ in World Christianity" Thangaraj helps us appreciate the progressive stages of *dislocation, disillusionment,* and *discernment* through which students tend to move when confronted with the realities of profound cultural and contextual differences in something so basic to Christian faith as the conceptualization of Christ. In moving through these phases students are coming to see themselves and understand their faith in new ways; they are learning to engage in contextual theological thinking.

One prominent strategy for contextualizing theological learning is that of integrating ecclesial practices as classroom pedagogy. In their chapter on "Christian Practices and Feminist Theological Formation," Joy McDougall, a systematic theologian, and Claire Bischoff, a religious educator, provide keen insights from their experimentation with integrating religious practices into their pedagogy while co-teaching a doctrine of God course focused on historical women's theological traditions and recent contemporary feminist and womanist discourse. McDougall and Bischoff argue that the effort to bridge "the artificial gap that exists between the teaching of doctrine and students' formation in Christian practices in seminary education" was particularly apropos of the women's historical traditions focused on in their course. But this chapter also illumines, via discussion of surprising successes as well as unexpected challenges, ways that religious practices may be engaged with integrity in an academic classroom and may enhance both practical and theoretical knowledge.

Contextualization is always a two-way street: it entails intentional efforts to extend learning beyond the classroom into relevant contexts in "the real world," and it also entails bringing realities of those extra-academic contexts into the classroom. Indeed, as Brent A. Strawn argues in his chapter on "Contemporary (Pop-)Cultural Contexts and the Old Testament Classroom," one does not really need to "bring the external world into the classroom" because it is always already there in the minds and views of students (and teachers) whose visions, stories, and myths have been thoroughly informed by the canons of contemporary popular culture. The real task, Strawn argues, is to convince students shaped by pop-culture that the theological content of a seminary course "has bearing on what they already believe to be true and how they enact such truth." Through examples from a course on the Bible and poetry, Strawn provides powerful critiques of pornography and violence in contemporary culture and shows how contextualization of a course makes theological education "public theology" in explicit relationship with real public realities.

While ecclesial practices may be engaged to stimulate integrative learning in the academic classroom, academic practices may also be engaged to stimulate integrative learning in the church. Another approach to contextualization is that of modeling in the classroom ecclesial practices meant to transform both classroom and church by promoting the integration of academic practices as transformative ecclesial practices. Luke Timothy Johnson here recounts his attempts in introductory New Testament courses to create constructive mutual interplay between academic and ecclesial practices and contexts. In describing "exegesis as an ecclesial practice" Johnson wishes to contend that "if it is the church as church that interprets Scripture, and if the church as a community of readers is itself always diverse and culturally conditioned, then the exegesis of the New Testament is inevitably and irreducibly contextual as well." This chapter describes a pedagogy honed over thirty years of teaching to fit a developing vision of "biblical exegesis as a practice of the church."

In the final chapter, Mary Elizabeth Moore draws on twenty-five years of experience in teaching and contextualizing in seminary classrooms to provide reflections on central issues in contextual education as well as delineate challenges for future directions and practices. With the keen eye of a veteran theologian and religious educator, Moore highlights a series of pedagogically rich cases from Claremont School of Theology and Candler School of Theology to glean insights, issues, and visions from her shared efforts in contextualizing theological education. Looking toward the future of theological education, the chapter concludes with extended reflections on and clues for pursuing contextual directions and contextual practices.

As Moore's concluding pages make evident, contextualizing theological education opens exciting new possibilities for theological teaching and learning, even as it also opens new questions about the meanings, intentions, and future directions of theological education as such. We hope the present volume contributes to this task and we look forward to continuing our participation in this important work.

*Part One*

# Context and Contextualization in Theological Education

# Chapter 1

# Theological Reflection in Contextual Education

## AN ELUSIVE PRACTICE

### *Elizabeth M. Bounds*

### *Two Scenes from a Contextual Education Reflection Seminar*

*Scene One — Three Weeks Into the Fall Semester*

"I can't figure Augustine out at all!"

"Me neither. I just read those words and they don't make any sense."

"Augustine just goes on and on about sin, but I don't know what he's talking about."

I am sitting in our third meeting of the weekly reflection seminar for Contextual Education I, listening to a litany of student sorrows and expressions of incomprehension and confusion. I feel a mixture of emotions: irritation (why don't they *try* harder?), sympathy (these first-year students have so much to take in this first semester — a new school, a new vocation, and a food cooperative that is the primary "context" of this course), and responsibility (what can I possibly do in the next two hours that can help them strengthen the connections between what happens in the classroom and their own sense of ministry?).

Today's session focuses on school as a context and is titled "What Is Theological Education All About?" The students have been assigned a short essay written in a personal style that addresses the challenges of moving from "words" to experienced ministry and have also been asked to look at the overall requirements they face to complete the M.Div. degree. We've started out the session by checking in on their student experience so far. Our conversation has stuck on the introductory historical theology course that almost all of them are taking.

I decide to try to work further with Augustine, clearly the source of much emotion at the moment, since he is currently being discussed in the historical theology course. What do you think he is saying about sin? I ask. Why does he insist upon the freedom of the human will? Do you believe you have free will? For many in the class, even though the words on the page are in English, they are trying to translate, so that little phrases, possibly phrases from their class lecture, pop up — "sin as separation," "original sin" — but when I press them to give examples, to use these phrases, there is a nervous blankness or a retreat into an expression of how they felt in a particular moment of their lives. They clearly found, with Kathleen Norris, that "the heavyweight theological words were a code I could not crack."[1]

Finally, I say, you need to think about what your theological bookcase looks like. They look at me, obviously confused. I go on: you are being given all these books, that is, ideas from Christian tradition, but if you don't have the shelves built and some sense of how you want these ideas ordered on these shelves, you won't be able to sort through all of this information and store it in places where you can find it again if you need it. This ordering system is yours; it's simply *your* theological questions. You need to see if Augustine is answering some of the theological questions you already have!

A few nod. A few look confused. I suspect they feel that the gap between Augustine's questions and theirs is so great that no bridge is possible. Or else their theological questions are so vague that they don't really know how to flesh them out, to find the more particular words that will help them build their theological bookcase.

---

1. Kathleen Norris, *Amazing Grace: A Vocabulary of Faith*, 221.

## Scene Two – Near the End of the Spring Semester

We are discussing the life of one of the members of their Contextual Education site — a food cooperative working out of a Baptist church that is trying to support and empower members, starting with organizing around the provision of food. In the previous semester, each student had met weekly with a cooperative member and had written a life history on the basis of their conversations. Paired with the particular life history for this week is a chapter from Howard Thurman's *Jesus and the Disinherited.* I have chosen Thurman because he does theology so deeply from the social and existential challenges that surround him. I am hoping his more accessible language will provide an easier entry point than Augustine for theological reflection.

We consider how Thurman's words speak to the life experience of the woman in the story who is a person with, to use Thurman's language, her "back constantly against the wall."[2] For him, the good news of Jesus can enable these disinherited, impoverished persons to escape "fear, hypocrisy, and hatred, the three hounds of hell."[3] The life we are engaging has included loss of vision, suicidal depression, bad relationships, poverty, discrimination, and endless hard work. Yet this woman affirms that God has been good to her, that Christ helps her see beyond herself. I ask how has she escaped the bitterness Thurman describes as "sustained resentment which is bottled up until it distills an essence of vitality" so that hatred becomes the basis of one's identity.[4] How does she understand Christian love?

The conversation is varied, flickering. Given the time of year, I am not sure who actually has done the reading since in the inevitable triage system of academic survival, the work for this pass/fail course tends to slide down the list of student priorities. I notice how many of the students frame the context in a completely individualistic way, thinking only of personal family history. They don't seem to see the relevance of the broader social and historical context that frames this woman's life — for example, she came to Atlanta from South Carolina as part of the exodus of many African Americans from rural to urban contexts, particularly in the post–civil rights era. Changes

2. Howard Thurman, *Jesus and the Disinherited*, 13.
3. Ibid., 29
4. Ibid., 79.

in city structure and in government welfare and disability programs have shaped this woman's resources and possibilities. Those who do name structures have difficulty talking about these institutional forces in relation to theology. I press a bit, asking how Thurman's christology may frame his understanding of suffering and survival and how that understanding might help us reflect upon this woman's life. Some students speak passionately from their experience of the site while others give fine accounts of the text. But almost none of them can link text and experience, enabling Thurman's words to speak to the situation.

## *What Is the Problem?*

I present these vignettes as a frame for a brief exploration of what I find to be some challenges of theological reflection as part of the work of contextual education. One of the major goals of the reflection seminars of both years of our program has been to reflect theologically *in context*, that is, reflecting on theological questions that have arisen from the sites, whether in a prison, a hospital, or a congregation. Yet throughout my work with our Contextual Education Program, both in leading seminars and planning the curriculum,[5] I have been confused over just what theological reflection is, how it relates to the theological curriculum, and how can it be taught.

I have come to see that "theological reflection" is a "weasel word," that is, an evasive term covering over difficult and challenging issues. I have found that using this phrase among theological faculty is comparable to using the phrase "Jesus Christ" with my seminarians — everyone relaxes since we presumably all know what it means and all agree it is central. The problem I have is that I do *not* think we know what it means — or at least we do not agree about what it means. The term "theological reflection" covers a range of knowledges, skills, and practices that can vary according to the theological assumptions and commitments of those seeking definition.

---

5. Since the Contextual Education Program was started in fall 1997, I have served both as a co-leader of student groups and, from 2002 to 2004, as chair of the faculty committee for the program. During the time I was chair, a faculty colleague and I tried to revise the basic curriculum for the two years of the program, an experience that catalyzed my need to become clearer about theological reflection.

1 □ 1 C

A red 1 □

B leaf C □ 1 X

1 □

G wh 4 □ R

This present essay is an effort to think through a few of the problems inherent in theological reflection (not the least of which is an effort to clarify what we mean by the term) and begin to suggest some ways to provide better work in such reflection as part of contextual education. In the rest of this essay, I will first attempt to unpack some of the components of theological reflection to suggest what a complex process it really is and that is thus requires much practice as part of a seminary education. I will then focus upon the particular problem I have faced in our contextual education work, namely, how to help students begin to practice or practice more richly the dialogue between theology and context that is at the heart of theological reflection. As a result of this brief discussion, I will finally suggest the challenges this work poses to the overall curriculum and the way these impact theological education, starting with the point that we may be doing everyone a disservice by seeing our goal as developing "theological reflection." I use some material from the Carnegie Endowment comparative study *Educating Clergy* to support the broader implications of my particular experiences.

## *Defining Theological Reflection*

I start with a simple description of theological reflection: engaging an experience or event in light of faith traditions in dialogue with one's personal experiences and an assessment of the context that surrounds both the event and the self.[6] Thus, at its core, theological reflection involves a triadic relationship of the Person(s) experiencing, the Situation or that which is being experienced, and the Theological Framework(s) used to assess what is being experienced.

While this framework is simple enough, actually engaging all three dimensions is hard work. First there is the challenge of assessing one's self and one's personal reactions and commitments with honesty and clarity. It is all too easy for such discernment to fall into what Richard

---

6. This simplified model is similar to the one offered by Patricia O'Connell Killen and John De Beer in *The Art of Theological Reflection*. However, while they use the category of experience (which, to them, includes lived narrative, culture, tradition, and positions or beliefs), I am using person and situation to emphasize the interactive moment of reflection located within a set of social and cultural structures (situation). See Killen and De Beer, *The Art of Theological Reflection*, esp. 53–61.

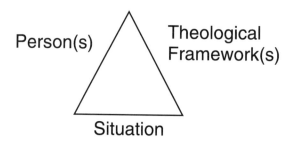

A Simple Diagram of Theological Reflection

Gula calls "moral myopia," the failure to see fully all the aspects involved in a situation.[7] If you have any doubts about the power of this myopia, a viewing of any broadcast of the *Dr. Phil* show will provide ample evidence as you watch persons denying actions and words already videotaped in their efforts to maintain their positive sense of their own goodness.

Then, there is the difficulty of assessing and engaging theological traditions, which requires not simply basic knowledge of history and doctrines but a sense of tradition as lived and living, as something directly affecting the ways we see the world. To do this well requires assessing both the relevant theological questions and the relevant resources within Christian traditions. Although I was convinced that all of my students had burning theological questions that were connected to the reading and the discussion, I found it hard to get them to frame these questions, let alone search for resources in what seemed to most of them to be distant and alien writings. Instead they were quick to fall back on what Patricia Killen and John De Beer call "religious code language,"[8] a formulaic incantation of theological words that keeps the question at a shallow level and never is able to dip deeper into the resources of traditions.

Then, finally, there is the challenge of assessing the experience or the situation, and trying to understand as fully as possible all of the dynamics at work. To return to my class, for example, it was very difficult for some of the students not only to grasp the multiplicity of

---

7. Richard M. Gula, *Moral Discernment*, 49.
8. Patricia Killen and John De Beer, *The Art of Theological Reflection*, 135.

factors creating poverty (government programs, employment possibilities, racial opportunities, urban planning, legal changes, etc.) but also to understand how these structures could be discerned in the life of a given individual and how both they and those on the site are enmeshed in such structures.

Theological reflection means performing an integrated analysis of self, theology, and situation. Depending on the reflection situation, different points of this triad are highlighted or merged, but what is key for learning is that all three dimensions are engaged and interacting. In contextual theological education, students are asked to make theological sense of what is happening right here, right now, in the lives and worlds around them. Many of our teaching problems arise when the relationship among the dimensions is not maintained, so that reflection falls apart into unrelated components. Each of the two scenes recounted above reflects a different version of this breakdown. The first illustrates the problem of a disjunction between the Christian tradition and the self of the student, the second a disjunction of theological framework and social context. In each case, the inability to use one side diminished the engagement with other two sides. Thus in the second example, the inability to deeply engage the context reduced the quality and depth of theological engagement possible and limited the possibility of personal growth in understanding.

In their contextual education experience, the students find themselves grappling with the two sides of the reflection triangle that appear to be "outside" of themselves: theology and context. Working with these sides requires two sets of "foreign" tools — the tools of social analysis and the tools of theological analysis. However, first-year students have little theological vocabulary, especially vocabulary rooted in Christian traditions. While they are beginning to get vocabulary in the introductory historical theology course, the classroom experience in these scenes is really their first chance to practice this vocabulary, to claim it and make it their own. And while the tools of theological analysis are being taught in many places in the curriculum, the tools of social analysis usually are not,[9] so that the seminar

---

9. This lack, evident in most seminaries, is connected to the observation made in Foster et al., *Educating Clergy,* that "we did not meet any seminary educators. . . . whose teaching practices explicitly engaged students in activities focused on *the systemic social transformation*

is not only a place for practicing knowledge acquired elsewhere in the curriculum, but a place for acquiring new knowledge through some rudimentary introduction to social analysis. When you add on the pressure of multiple commitments and psychological challenge of first year of seminary, it is hardly surprising that so many of them quickly fall back onto the side they know best, themselves and their experience, when they cannot figure out how to find and use the tools they need for a deeper analysis.

## *Teaching Possibilities*

Given the analysis I have just made, I find a central pedagogical challenge for the contextual education classroom is to develop learning experiences that enable students to practice working with all three dimensions so that they can integrate personal experience, cognitive understandings of tradition, and contextual analysis in reflection and in action. Ideally, this class would assign very little reading but instead focus upon assignments and in-class work that draw upon both the experience at the site and upon readings the students currently are doing in other classes or have already done.[10] The focus of any reading assigned would be teaching skills of social analysis, the skills that the students are not likely to be getting anywhere else in their theological education.[11] Examples include:

- Double-entry journals in which students keep a journal from their site work on half the page and consider connections to some of the readings in other courses or some of the readings in social analysis on the other half of the page. These are building block assignments

---

*of institutions or systems"* (151, italics in text). Tools of social analysis are a prerequisite for any kind of systemic work.

10. Candler will soon find out whether this structure would be helpful since we are about to implement changes to the format of this first-year Contextual Education course that require a first year M.Div. student to take an Arts of Ministry course in the fall, which will be linked with their contextual site.

11. Unfortunately, there are few resources that provide these skills. A classic text is Joe Holland and Peter Henriot, *Social Analysis: Linking Faith and Justice,* but it is a bit dated. A more recent, clearly written analysis of urban poverty by David Hilfiker, *Urban Injustice: How Ghettos Happen,* can be used as an example of social analysis with the skills deductively developed. Some elementary sociology texts can also be helpful.

that can be the background or foundation for some of the more developed assignments mentioned below.

- In-class writings on theological topics in relationship to a discussion of an issue arising at the site.

- An assignment explaining a theological concept from the perspective of a person at the site.

- A sermon outline or Bible study plan designed for the site, with a brief explanation of the purpose or focus in relation to the site context.

- Regular "critical incidents" where students write up a site encounter with a paragraph on the social and theological concerns at stake (these incidents could be reflected on in class not only through discussion but through role play).

There are a few essential considerations. One is that the assignments must be limited, focused, and repeated to give the students the chance to practice one small piece of what is a very large set of skills, practices, etc. (e.g., pastoral leadership). A second consideration is that preparing these assignments and in-class exercises requires both knowledge of the theological curriculum and knowledge of the context/site, thus requiring a close collaboration between the teaching faculty person and the person responsible for supervision at the site. Finally, it is important to keep reminding students of the purpose of the particular exercise, including relating it to the "big picture" of theological reflection and pastoral understanding, a picture that is incomplete without social analysis.

## *Curricular Challenge*

My triangle of theological reflection is, of course, ridiculously simplified. Any such model or diagram is at best a heuristic device, helping us sort out the "buzzing blooming confusion" that is everyday reality. For example, my beliefs are already profoundly shaped by my own context and formation in theological traditions that may or may not be significantly different from the context of situation so that I need to do structural analysis of my own location in relationship to the person, event, or situation, I am trying to engage. Thus, if I were more skilled at diagramming, I would try to map a triangle onto a multidimensional context. But even that would be inadequate as it leaves the work of reflection as a frozen, static moment. But this reflective work is hardly static; it is an ongoing process of reflection/action/reflection.

We need to consider what we are calling theological reflection as "knowing in action,"[12] seeing it as a form of practical reasoning or *phronesis*. The terms "theological discernment" or "practical wisdom" might, in fact, be far better descriptions of this process.[13] Using the term "reflection" tends to privilege the phase of removed contemplation and analysis, the very phase that is most alienating to so many students. A time of removal is required, the separation of analysis, but academic coursework in seminaries tends to stress that separation to the extent that students cannot reintegrate.[14] Fieldwork or contextual education are the curricular places where integration is supposed to occur but as the authors of *Educating Clergy* put it, "the mutuality of *techne* and *phronesis* at the center of the interdependence of the cognitive, skill, and professional identity apprenticeships has often been pedagogically elusive in seminary field education programs."[15]

The overall goal of theological education is to foster this kind of "knowing in action," a process that requires a variety of learning experiences including knowledge acquisition, skills development, and personal formation. These experiences are the key components of the three main apprenticeships — cognitive, practical, and normative — which the authors of *Educating Clergy* see as foundational to

---

12. Donald A. Schön, *Educating the Reflective Practitioner*, 25.

13. Another term, suggested by Craig Dykstra, is "pastoral imagination." In *Vision and Discernment: An Orientation in Theological Study*, Charles Wood defines discernment as the "effort to grasp and assess what is really there in the situation" (73).

14. One influential analysis of this problem is found in Edward Farley, *Theologia: The Fragmentation and Unity of Theological Education*. An analysis that frames the question in a social and historical context can be found in William M. Sullivan, *Work and Integrity: The Crisis and Promise of Professionalism in America*, 227–56.

15. Foster et al., *Educating Clergy: Teaching Practices and the Pastoral Imagination*, 320.

theological education.[16] Every course at seminary provides a component of one or more of these apprenticeships, the building blocks for students to use.

However, the term "apprenticeship" suggests an active process requiring what William Sullivan calls an "intimate pedagogy of modeling and coaching."[17] While preparation for the profession of ministry has preserved more of this intimacy than the preparation of doctors or lawyers, we still are challenged to think through these pedagogies, especially those of us who work in a university context where isolated analytic knowledge, separated by guild, is particularly valued. The pedagogies must not only be intimate, they also must be based upon an understanding of the overall curriculum and its purposes. As *Educating Clergy* notes, one of the major challenges that theological education faces is not merely training persons in the different apprenticeships but helping them "align" the apprenticeships, enabling them to bring those skills, knowledges, and experiences together.[18]

As I have reflected upon the challenges I have experienced in the Contextual Education classroom, I have come to see my efforts at encouraging theological reflection as one of the first places in their seminary work where students can begin to practice this "alignment." I have also recognized that such alignment requires an understanding of the school, its curriculum, and the content and pedagogies of its various courses (particularly those that are part of a mandatory core). Such understanding is a steep learning curve for many faculty. For example, some of the work I sketched above requires me to know both *what* texts and ideas my colleagues in systematic and historical theology are teaching and *how* they are being taught.

Theological reflection is foundational to the work of theological education. I believe it is not really reflection, but, rather theology-in-action, dependent upon the richness of our multiple interactions: faculty with the curricula, students with texts and contexts, faculty with students, students with students, faculty with faculty. Such

---

16. See ibid., 25.
17. Sullivan, *Work and Integrity*, 195.
18. "Alignment" is a term borrowed from H. Gardner et al., *Good Work: Where Excellence and Ethics Meet* (see Foster et al., *Educating Clergy*, 298).

interactions will foster skills and practices of listening, analyzing, and reflecting on the part of both students and faculty. Theological schools that are committed to developing these interactions and practices will need to intentionally devote time to common reflective work by faculty so that there is shared understanding, indeed ownership, of the curriculum.[19] In other words, if we faculty are to be engaged in contextual education, requiring students to work deeply out of their context, we have to work just as deeply ourselves.

---

19. Given the burden of work already undertaken by faculty, I should emphasize that shared understanding does not necessarily imply shared implementation. For example, Candler has had a long commitment to participation by all faculty in providing contextual education. But my work in our program has shown me that faculty have different pedagogical skills and resources so it is not educationally valuable for every faculty person to participate in exactly the same way.

# Chapter 2

# Origins of Contextualization in the Global Church

*W. Harrison Daniel*

Stephen Bevans wrote the book on Contextualization — literally. His 1992 work, entitled *Models of Contextual Theology,* posits boldly in his first sentence: "There is no such thing as theology; there is only contextual theology: feminist theology, black theology, liberation theology, Filipino theology, Asian American theology, African theology and so forth."[1] Bevans explores the contours of a number of different contextual theological models, but traces the origins of the term "contextualization" in the important work of a now somewhat obscure Taiwanese theological educator: Shoki Coe.

Shoki Coe (Taiwanese name, C. H. Hwang, 1914–88) developed the notion of contextual theology that was adopted by the World Council of Churches in its work promoting global theological education: the Theological Education Fund (TEF). In the TEF annual report to the WCC meeting in 1972, Coe unveiled a compelling vision of what he termed "contextual theology." He proposed a new way of doing theology well beyond the Western dominated models of translating old inherited theological concepts for the Third World. He articulated a theological move towards the autonomy of pre-Christian religious and philosophical traditions to ask questions of Christianity, as well as putting questions to churches from the rapid changes in global economic and political integration. Coe thereby shaped his concepts based on his work aligning Presbyterian theological education to both local and global issues affecting his native

---

1. Stephen B. Bevans, *Models of Contextual Theology,* 3.

Formosa, later to become known as Taiwan, after the deposed Kuomintang party retreated there from China when the Communists won the Chinese Civil War in 1949. Furthermore, through the auspices of the WCC Coe's work has served and shaped both international and domestic theological education for thirty-five years. In an era when theological education is challenged to become more international in all settings by global shifts of gravity towards the Southern church, as well as by national accrediting agencies such as the Association of Theological Schools (ATS), revisiting the international yet indigenously relevant origins of contextualization in Coe's work in the pluralist theological setting of Taiwan holds exciting possibilities for the challenges and prospects of doing contextual theology and revitalizing pastoral education wherever seminaries are facing "glocal" pluralist social locations. And where in the world is the local church not faced with such global challenges?

Born in 1914 into a family where his father and grandfather before him were ministers of the Presbyterian Church of Taiwan, C. H. Hwang was schooled in the fine Taiwan Presbyterian educational institutions in Tainan and Taipei. He was further exposed to global Christian scholarship while studying in Tokyo, Birmingham, England, and finally taking a degree in theology from Westminster College, Cambridge, in 1941. Unable to return home because of World War II, Coe taught Japanese at the University of London during the war. Returning to Taiwan in 1947, he took over presidential leadership of an almost defunct Bible school. From 1949 to 1965, Coe led the deeply influential Tainan Theological College to become one of Asia's premier theological college and research centers, devoted to deep immersion into the Taiwanese religious past and political independence from China.

Coe authentically combined contrasting cultural traits. He picked up quite a repertoire of skills from his years abroad in Japan and Britain. He took the name Shoki Coe to indicate how the colonial powers Japan and Great Britain marked him. Coe effortlessly embraced many contrasts. A brilliant intellectual, Coe was both fearless and charming. He was a visionary about theology and its place in relation to local culture and globalization. Yet he was an effective and pragmatic administrator. A true citizen of the world and a committed international diplomat, he was also fiercely protective of the culture and political future of Taiwan over against China. Rock-hard in persuasiveness, Coe possessed a warm and gentle Christian faith, guided by true theological depth.

Forced into political exile due to his support for Taiwanese independence from China, Coe found himself homeless. As a refugee of Asian colonialism, he embarked upon an international journey of education and service. Coe's wide cultural and religious experiences, along with his innate diplomatic skills, led him in 1965 to become the director of the WCC Theological Education Fund/Program for Theological Education, which he led until 1979. In this position, Coe was able to translate his theological convictions into a program that promoted indigenous pastoral education for the emerging and fast growing non-Western churches around the globe. To this end, Coe's life and work came together in the important concept of contextualizing theology. In the TEF report (*Ministry in Context: The Third Mandate Programme of the Theological Education Fund (1970–72)*, unveiled at the TEF's 1972 meeting, Shoki Coe described the need to get beyond indigenizing Western theology for non-Western theological contexts. Instead, he clearly argued for the dynamic interplay between the religio-cultural past and the rapid social changes of non-Western contexts, in order to become the authentic starting point for contextual theology. His ideas became a rallying cry for those seeking a place for theology in promoting self-determination among the newly decolonized independent countries and their intelligentsia — ironically often produced by church education programs. Coe wrote with a passion about the need for church leaders and their theology to be midwives to positive political, social, and economic change in a rapidly changing global landscape. He defined his ideas in an abstract from his article "Contextualizing Theology":

> In the developing theologies of the "younger churches" in the Third World, the emphasis has shifted from indigenization to contextualization. Why? How do they differ? Indigenization derives from the idea of "taking root in the soil," and tends to suggest a static response to the Gospel in terms of traditional

culture. Therefore, it is in danger of being past-oriented. The context today, however, is not that of static culture, but the search for the new, which at the same time has involved the culture itself. In using the word "contextualization," we try to convey all that is implied in the familiar term "indigenization," yet seek to press beyond for a more dynamic concept which is open to change and that is also future-oriented.[2]

Before Coe's TEF report, the issue of a missionary engagement with Gospel and Culture had been framed in terms of indigenization.[3] Growing out of the Three-Self principle of Rufus Anderson, Henry Venn, and John Nevious in the mid-nineteenth century, the notion that a church should be self-supporting, self-propagandizing, and self-led carried over into notions that Western church models must be planted and adapted in the soil of local culture. Yet the model did not address the need for self-theologizing and, by extension, a culturally relevant theological education for local pastoral leadership. The fourth self — self-theologizing — was necessary for every healthy church to avoid the theological script coming from the outside and the past.[4] While this may seem tame and even obvious now, we do well to revisit Coe's ideas and push them to question our own use of contextual theology, particularly where we train pastors to bridge the gap between text and context.

## Implications of Coe's Contextualization Theory: Applications for a "Glocal" Theology

Coe's writing capitalized on the need for theological education to be located more centrally among the vital, emergent non-Western churches during the postcolonial era. In this phase, local culture and religious dialogue were beginning to be taken seriously, but were also being pushed by global issues and "signs of the times." Commentators have coined a term for this kind of theology and practice, as "glocal" — in that theology and theological education should be

---

2. Shoki Coe, "Contextualizing Theology," 33–34.
3. H. C. Chua, "Hermeneutical Concerns in Contextualization," 2–3.
4. Wilbert R. Shenk, *Changing Frontiers of Mission*, 53.

done in view of the increasing connections between the global and the local. In fact a theology that plays merely at one end of these poles is dangerously divorced from the world. According to Coe, without referencing the universal and the local impinging upon one another, there can be no genuine and liberating changes to usher in a future of hope to transform the past and present.[5] Thus, there are "authentic and false forms of contextualization":

> False Contextualization yields to uncritical accommodation [of the churches], a form of culture faith. Authentic contextualization is always prophetic, arising always out of a genuine encounter between God's Word and his world, and moves toward the purpose of challenging and changing the situation through rooted-ness in and commitment to a given historical moment.[6]

Thus for Coe, there are real implications for doing this kind of theology and putting it to the service of theological education. He argued that theology could define what is timeless, transcendent, and universal about Christian faith and practice only when it addresses a particular time, place, and culture. Indeed Coe discerned that the incarnation of Christ points us in a direction: the Universal Logos takes form in a particular person, a culture, a time, and place.[7] In this act, the transcendent is translated as a Jewish man named Jesus, born in first-century Palestine, who wanders in a Roman imperial occupied land and preaches the arrival of a different future in God's Reign. Defining Jesus as God incarnate is the ultimate translation. Furthermore, each faith community as it develops its theology, practices, and prophetic action is thus in this view a retranslation of the life of God in Christ. In more traditional terms, this contextualization is at the heart of our common life.

These implications in Coe's work offer exciting ways to reformulate the faith afresh. For those committed to practicing the faith in

---

5. Shoki Coe, "In Search of Renewal in Theological Education," 241–42.
6. World Council of Churches, *Ministry in Context: The Third Mandate Programme of the Theological Education Fund*, 20; Coe was the principal author of this document.
7. Ray Wheeler, "The Legacy of Shoki Coe," 179.

a rapidly globalizing, pluralistic world, Coe's work shows the fallacy of playing local theology against universal theology. The choice for him is not between maintaining faithfulness to a tradition and forming contemporary attitudes in our students. As Coe so helpfully articulated, the curricular and pedagogical choices are not between a contextual vs. catholic (universal) theology. Rather, we develop a truly universal theology precisely when we are most committed to doing theology in, for, and through the context for a prophetic transformation. Thereby we root and "re-root" our traditions in the life of religious and cultural change and thus find guidance to act creatively in hope for a different future: health for people, communities, cultures, and our globe.

Contextualization in Coe's thought takes us to the heart of key practices for pastors and the communities they serve: (1) the faithful and creative transmission of biblical faith in a pluralist culture with multiple languages; (2) the appropriation and reformulation of that faith in real persons and communities for the sake of meeting and transforming the world.

Let us look deeper at contextualization in terms of these practices and suggest how Coe's work continues to inform those engaged in a pastoral formation that seeks to be faithful and yet contemporary. The following section represents an intersection of Coe's seminal thought and my reading of his work, particularly as it relates to contextual theological education.

Coe developed three important categories of theological discourse that should inform effective training for pastoral leadership and the transmission of the faith. Each of these categories shapes transmission of the faith and seminary pedagogy and should be the subjects that organize a new view of time, cultural identity, and space in view of Christ's incarnation.

## *Eschatology (New Time)*

Coe began his theological assessments by paying attention to the eschatological dimension as the promise of a new approach to the future. Coe looked at the political oppression and violence of the middle third of the twentieth century and found it irresponsible not to comment on the apparently tenuous relationship of the failed past and the brokenness of the present to the eschatological promises of the future. He expressed this in terms of living in the tension of the "present and not yet," while receiving glimpses of the future through actions that demonstrate the "fullness of time" already dawning. Out of this came his notion of the task of the church and the kinds of practices its leaders should engage in. If God entered time through Jesus Christ, this ultimate contextualization creates the dawning of a New Time, filled with promise of a different, better future. Old Time — the terror of meaningless cycles — is over. Coe affirms that Christ has entered time, and so has brought the divine purpose into history once and for all time. Therefore we witness to this New Time and act in hope for the time when all creation is fulfilled in Christ. Christians cannot hide; we are impelled to be where Christ is, in time, working and witnessing so that the future order is concretely felt in the present.[8]

Indeed, Coe's notion of contextualism is clearly distinguished for its future orientation. He wanted to contrast contextualization from indigenization: an older concept of cross-cultural ministry derived from translating static, past-oriented communication of the Gospel in categories heavily impressed with Western epistemological assumptions, namely, that non-Western cultures do not develop rapidly. Rather, Coe pointed out that non-Western cultures and Christian churches there are undergoing rapid change. Static and perhaps outdated notions of traditional cultures cannot uncritically shape Christian theology and foundations for ministry. Rather, the "context" in contextualization is the "search for the new," not simply for the sake of hearing something new, but to hear the Gospel in the new worlds emerging through the globalization of economics and communication. Indeed, Coe could not have dreamed how much the digital era would change global patterns of interaction, identity, and community. Yet his call for contextualization as a "search for the new," as a way to communicate the Gospel in view of changing interactions between the local and the global, appears prescient today. It is a call for leadership formation that requires nothing less than telling the

---

8. Ibid., 79.

old story of Jesus to a new global audience, but with local accents and assumptions. This becomes the global church communities' task together, lest we miss the dynamic connection between the chaotic present and the kairotic future, due to the brokenness of any one culture's broken church history. Moreover, this task — developing contextual theology to nurture local church communities — is a necessary, if not sufficient, condition for the global church to live its existence as a cross-temporal witness to the Eschaton. Training Christian leaders by paying attention to the diverse interactions between the global and local voices of Christian communities becomes the priority theological agenda for the future. For as Coe argues, this is simply "the missiological discernment of the signs of the times, seeing where God is at work and calling us to participate in it." Such themes should guide the actions and accents of our transmission of the faith. Moreover, taking Coe's ideas seriously for curricular and pedagogical choices, we should continue to maximize exposure to diverse global and local expressions of the faith, to meet the "glocal" mission challenges of our time.

## Context (New Identity)

Through his years of studying and working abroad, as well as his political exile, Coe saw himself through multiple identities (and names). Living among the global church leadership at the WCC and living his faith among people of other cultures, he was sensitive to the power of culture and language to shape religious identity. In this regard, he wrote: "[National and Cultural identity] determines the basic structures and general style of life in society as a whole, and so becomes its coordinating principle." But Shoki Coe was no cultural determinist. He quickly added, "To be faithful to its call, the church must not shirk its God-given gift to live and work in the very heart of this new social revolution. . . . For God to love the entire community of man in all its confusing multiplicity does not mean that everything is equally acceptable to Him as an expression of His will."[9]

---

9. C. H. Hwang, *Joint Action for Mission in Formosa: A Call for Advance into a New Era.*

As the quote indicates, Coe strongly delineated the freedom all humans have to fulfill the Missio Dei. Proclamation attentive to human demography came to be seen by Coe as an important sign of God's mission producing a New Humanity. To this degree, Coe saw population and demographic statistics as important, because they stood for persons for whom Christ died. As a theological educator, he taught his students that statistics were not just a U.S. American or Western biased account of religious significance; rather, they provided clues to two important aspects forming Christian identity in every time and place: the necessary reflection upon the history of a culture and its Christian roots, along with how the changing context reshapes connections between the past and the future. Demographics offered a glimpse into the shape of human identities and communities to come. Moreover, demographics posed and answered questions about which factors prompted growth in faith and which factors provided natural limits. Such dynamics became important markers that needed attention in a seminary curriculum capable of training leaders to speak to global and local pressures.

Coe was realistic in seeing that the Taiwanese Church of the 1950s–1970s had some political and sociological limits. Clearly it was marked by a peculiar sense of isolationism, irrelevance to the culture, elitism, class stratification, and even exploitation of the poor. Coe was clear as the preeminent leader of the Presbyterian Church in Taiwan that his church was not fully reflective of the New Humanity or New Creation. Nor is there any church in any culture fully representative of God's perfected future people. To make this point clear, Coe used the illustration that contextualization is analogous to the operation of a lighthouse. As Ray Wheeler documents the analogy, "The church had to lead in direct involvement in the community rather than attempting to pull a few individuals out of the community into a structure designed just for them. The church cannot effectively contextualize its message if it caters to the temptation to withdraw from the challenge, to be content with the role of comfortable, middle-class, introverted religious clubs."[10]

---

10. Wheeler, "The Legacy of Shoki Coe," 80, n. 10.

In such forceful images, Coe called for Christians to engage the world. For Coe, discipleship shapes the future through relating the Word to the World. Posing prophetic questions back to the church commits Christians to a certain set of identity shifts. To walk with God through the world means to search for our identity and our place and how to reconcile the changing world with the eternal. But in Coe's contextualization, to find our place — our identity as people and individuals — means to discover ourselves over and over again. This is done through transmitting the tradition and translating it for new contexts. In the process, the Spirit will reinvent identities, relocate and reform communities, and even rename individuals (like Coe himself).

## *Catholicity (New Space)*

One of Coe's most important contributions to the WCC through the Theological Education Fund was his reflective work on criteria to assess variances in contexts in relation to the transcendent Word. It was an attempt to chart the connective relationships of individual cultural expressions of faith to larger, universal, transcendent themes. In a very real sense, Coe was drawing the "rose lines" that connected an emerging global Christianity in New Catholicity, and thereby transformed the planet into a new Okumene. On this topic, he suggested that context could not be reified, lest Christianity become merely a local product or identity marker. "To take the context seriously does not necessarily mean, it seems to me, taking all contexts equally seriously, because all are not equally strategic for the Missio Dei (Mission of God) in the working out of His purpose through history."[11] There were limits to contextualization. When context is the defining boundary of all that a Christian can say or know or accept, we have moved from Coe's contextualization to a mere contextualism. Coe recognized that theological training in the emerging global church required careful attention to the interrelationships between global and local realities, informing the witness and work of the church in the world.[12] Unless Christianity is universal with an impulse to move, to

---

11. Coe, *In Search of Renewal*, 239.
12. Ibid., 236.

connect, and to share its message, it becomes merely a local religion, a sort of totem pole reflection of a local culture or society.

At the heart of Coe's theological method is how he takes seriously the analogy between incarnation and contextualization. Indeed, Christianity, built on the divine translation affirmation at the heart of the incarnation can mean little to the world unless Christians get up, move, and practice their faith in connection with the world. Coe would not concur that "Demography is Destiny" — that religion is purely a function of ethnic determinism. For him, a Christianity that does not move among cultures and cross boundaries can lay little claim to being anything more than a civil or tribal religion. The phenomenal growth of Christianity and its shift of Christian gravity to the non-Western world — demographics only partially revealed by the time of Coe's death in 1988 — suggests that Coe's instincts were right: there is something in this missionary faith that is not dependent upon Western philosophy, capitalist economics, liberal democratic political constructs, or literate religious prehistories.

In his influential book *Constructing Local Theologies,* Robert Schreiter puts forth criteria to guard catholicity.[13] He does so in ways consistent with Coe's calls to root theology in local realities, while heeding Coe's warning against a false contextualism that promotes local realities over global Christian continuities. Genuine forms of theology that are "glocal" take context seriously to avoid a false Western dominance, yet also recognize theological continuities across culture and time. In order for local theologies to be legitimate in these ways, Schreiter names five criteria to query contextual theology: (1) Is the theology consistent internally, with all of its implications in basic harmony with the great central themes of the faith — such as justification by grace through faith? (2) Can the theology be translated into worship, giving rise to creative yet faithful liturgical expressions? (3) Does the theology lead to ortho-praxis, where ideas give rise to fruits in faithful action? (4) Does the theology enter into dialogue with other theologies and religious traditions, offering opportunities for sharpening in self-correction? (5) Does the theology have the strength to challenge and shape other religious ideas, revitalizing it

---

13. Robert Schreiter, *Constructing Local Theologies,* 117–21.

and other local theologies? Schreiter makes a strong case that these principles allow a theologian to take culture seriously, without taking culture more seriously than the Jewish and Christian traditions as expressed in Scripture and church tradition.[14] As a Catholic theologian, Schreiter shows a remarkable convergence with Presbyterian Coe's seminal thinking. This paradoxically demonstrates that doing contextual theology is an activity that transcends and unites Catholic and Protestant identities.

In this connection, Coe strongly maintained that contextualization was worth little if done in ignorance of the catholicity of the Gospel. He clearly recognized that rootedness and commitment to a given historical situation, without a catholicity linked to scriptural and vital unity, could devolve into a "chameleon theology" — changing its color to blend in and protect itself in a hostile environment. In an irony, Coe made a strong case that contextualization is the authentic way of achieving vital catholicity. He argued that it is precisely by taking the concrete situation seriously that contextual theology becomes truly catholic. Attention to the unique and the local growth of Christianity as it relates to a fast-changing environment translates the movement into a more universal and global presence. Coe redefined a contemporary, practical notion of catholicity: "True catholicity is not the same thing as colourless uniformity, bur rather a manifold and diverse theology which responds to a different context, just as the Incarnate Word did on our behalf, once and for all."[15] This has implications for seminary curriculum. Leaders of theological seminaries rapidly seeking to "go global" take note: seeking a quick catholicity (often translated as a "globalized" curriculum) to appease accrediting or grant-making agencies or appeal to a broader market simply cannot bypass the hard work of taking local contexts seriously. There is no catholicity for the church or its leadership that does not seek out new spaces to discover the relationship between Christ and Culture — places where we have both incarnated the Gospel in culture and incarcerated the Gospel within culture. This leads to asking questions about the compromising effect of powerful funding agencies on

---

14. Schreiter, *Constructing Local Theologies*, 121.
15. Shoki Coe, *Recollections and Reflections*, 274.

the ability for seminaries to authentically educate leaders, particularly as they serve the interests of the marginalized and the global poor — the kind of church Shoki Coe knew, served, and pointed toward prophetically.

## Conclusion: Shoki Coe's Legacies

Shoki Coe left behind many legacies after his death in 1988. Much of his best work was probably done in his teaching and leading Tainan Theological College in his beloved Taiwan. Coe lived in exile from 1965 until a year before his death in Britain. Perhaps his most fertile period is hidden from us, done in the crucible of reviving his seminary in the atmosphere of postwar Taiwan. Fortunately we have his mature reflections from the WCC and TEF years, which filtered his theological method honed in Taiwan and refracted it for the entire global church. Yet more work needs to be done connecting his WCC writings on contextual theology with how these ideas inform classroom pedagogy seeking to be "glocal." Within a decade of his coining and defining the concept of "contextualization," Coe's reflections had gained widespread currency among conciliar Protestants, while it would take Evangelicals a little longer to trust the term. Today, many contextual education, supervised ministry, and field education programs in North American Protestant seminaries employ some version of his theology of contextualization, though few directors of these programs have an understanding of the international, missiological, and ecumenical origins of the term. Shoki Coe's vision of contextual theology helped the WCC further stimulate a new catholicity: a catholicity that transforms the planet closer to the sacred space envisioned in Scripture — where the New Jerusalem will be the meeting place of God and the New Humanity, and where all the nations will bring their treasures (Rev. 22). In the meantime, the treasures found in contextual theology may still well serve theological education seeking to form creative and faithful leaders to serve their "glocal" communities. Shoki Coe's model of contextualization, therefore, offers those who design and teach theological education in a global key rich methods to better understand ourselves, our traditions, and our transcendent connections.

# Chapter 3

# Theological Thinking as Contextual Practice

*Theodore Brelsford and John Senior*

This chapter develops an understanding of skillful theological think-ing that builds on notions of "catching theology in action" and "reconstructing theology in practice." Catching theology in action en-tails examining one's own and others' actions in specific events and specific contexts in order to discern functional theological assump-tions informing those actions. Reconstructing theology in practice involves bringing existing theological assumptions into conversation with the theological assumptions and perspectives of others and of formal biblical and theological traditions. Our intent is to promote a particular way of conceiving theological thinking that implies and enables practices and processes for teaching contextual theological thinking in seminary or theology/divinity school classrooms.

As suggested in the title, our focus here is on theological thinking. This is not to eschew or devalue important and related concerns such as knowledge acquisition, professional and spiritual formation, and the like, but rather merely to delineate a manageable scope for this chapter and to identify what we see as a vital contextual educational concern. Central assumptions of this essay include: (1) thinking is a complex and often a vague notion; (2) thinking happens not in iso-lation, but in community; and (3) thinking is not *ex nihilo* ideation; rather, thinking is always a project of reconstruction of preexisting assumptions and perceptions formed from the material of tradition, history, and experience. While there are many contexts in which skill-ful theological thinking can happen, in this essay we attend to one in particular: the seminary classroom. In the first section below, on

"Thinking and Theology," we address the question of how students in seminary (or theology school or divinity school) classrooms may develop as skillful theological thinkers in ways that will serve them well in their ministry. In the second section, we examine more carefully the particular context of the classroom. Then, in the third section, we discuss the kind of contextualized theological thinking that can happen there. There we develop more fully our notion of skillful theological thinking by exploring notions of discernment, interpretation, and appropriation. In so doing, we assume a notion of practical theology that includes skillful theological thinking as a (re)constructive process of communal reflection on God's presence in human events. A classroom community can think together constructively in ways that are skillful and theological, and ways that engage both course material and the many experiences that students bring to the classroom. We aim to strengthen the ability of teachers to enhance such skillful contextual theological thinking.

## Thinking and Theology

A common mantra among theological faculty members and teaching supervisors who lead Contextual Education seminars is "we want students to learn how to think theologically." A common complaint among such seminar leaders, and also among some discerning students, is that even at the end of their second year of Contextual Education courses many students still don't do it well — they are not skillful in thinking theologically. Many of them are still unclear about what it really means to think theologically. Perhaps many faculty and supervisors are also unclear.

Part of the problem in understanding what it means to think theologically is that the terms "theology" and "thinking" have multiple, varied, and often diffuse meanings. There is formal, systematic, and constructive theology. There is theology as an intellectual activity of faith seeking understanding. There is theology as a practice of reflecting on experience in relation to theological assumptions and commitments. There is theology as worldview, and theology as faith doctrine, and so forth. This does not, of course, exhaust the possible ways of thinking about theology, and these ways are not all mutually exclusive. The point is that "theology" carries many and varied meanings and functions.

"Thinking" is even more difficult to pin down. Much modern educational theory is shaped by John Dewey's notion of thinking as problem solving. In this model thinking is paradigmatically the scientific method of developing and testing hypotheses about the world around us in order to formulate theories to guide and enrich future actions and experiences.[1] Another common contemporary model for thinking is the computer: thinking as information processing. In this model processing more information more quickly is always better than processing less information less quickly. Many of us may object that the human mind is not a computer. But there are prominent contemporary educational processes that, at least on the surface, look much like information processing — students read texts, absorb lectures, and churn out papers. The propensity to pack educational programs with more and more courses and requirements and objective learning measurement standards also indicates something like an information processing model. This is true in theological education as much as in other kinds of education.

There are ways of understanding processes of thinking that are more religious. For example, thinking may be understood as a discernment process — trying to find within the plethora of our sensory intake that which is useful and important, good and true and meaningful. Another religious conception of thinking is contemplation, which entails attending to things without engaging in problem solving and without trying to process information in a rational sense, and without moving too quickly to discernment — just attending. The point here is not to fully delineate the meanings of thinking theologically, but to make clear that there are a variety of such meanings for both terms.

In this chapter, we focus primarily on thinking theologically as processes of "catching theology in action" and "reconstructing theology in practice." In other words, theological thinking entails uncovering

---

1. John Dewey, *How We Think: A Restatement of the Relation of Reflective Thinking to the Educative Process.*

functional *assumptions* about God in ourselves, others, and institutions in order to consciously reform those assumptions in the context of a particular community of theological reflection. For those who wish to teach skills of theological thinking it is important to attend carefully both to processes of discernment (which we discuss in terms of "catching theology in action") and to processes of constructive thought formation (which we term "constructing theology in practice").

Thinking about the world theologically is sometimes conceived as primarily the discernment of God's activity and presence in the world, without adequately acknowledging the constructive nature of the knowledge produced out of discernment. When we ask, "Where is God in this event?" we are inviting discernment — discernment of the truth of God's presence and God's action in a particular event. But when we answer the question we are constructing provisional human understanding, not simply stating the truth we sought to discern. And when a community (a classroom, a congregation, a denomination) reaches some agreement about a particular understanding of God's presence and action in a particular event or in the world at large, then theological knowledge has been constructed — *we know* something about God in the world.

If we are not careful, construction can overwhelm discernment. Theological thinking is not simply a process of interpreting the world and human experiences in terms of established or developing theological conceptions. The focus on interpretation attends well to the constructive dimension of theological thinking, but may move too quickly to construction, thereby missing the need for faithful discernment of "what is" before constructing understanding of what it means. In short, discernment and construction are of a piece, and any model of skillful theological reflection must account for the complementary relationship between them.

Furthermore, theological thinking is necessarily a communal process. This may be more profoundly true than is commonly thought. We know that a wide array of environmental factors (social, economic, political) influence individual thinking. But more than just influencing the thinking of individuals, communities and societies and ecologies of all sorts also "think." In some of his later writings, for example, the anthropologist Gregory Bateson began to attribute the terms "mind" and "intelligence" to whole ecological systems. There is an intelligence that emerges in a pond, and in a forest, and in all organic systems, including especially human social systems. Bateson's work has been subsequently used by some educational theorists to think about ecologies of thinking and learning that are formed in classrooms and institutions and communities.[2] Ideas and ways of thinking emerge in a collective and are shaped by the unique persons and relationships within them and the environment around them, similar to ways that ideas and patterns of thinking emerge in an individual — shaped by the individual's unique genetic composition and experiences and social and environmental location. Ecology and community are vital dimensions of thinking, and they are present in the many contexts of theological reflection.

Finally, thinking theologically is a practice. As such, it has a skill set associated with it that we want students to develop and that we elaborate in the concepts of "catching theology in action" and "reconstructing theology in practice" (see below pp. 52ff.). Etienne Wenger argues that learning is not just a matter of mastering information, and knowledge is not merely the accumulation of data.[3] Instead, learning is deeply embedded in the practices of communities that try together to make sense of their world. Knowledge therefore is fundamentally rooted in the competences one develops in the meaning-making practices of a learning community rather than in the development of ideational structures in one's mind, as it were. Meaning happens in the dialectical movement between "participation" (engagement in community-shared and deeply embodied experiences that provide the raw material for reflection) and "reification" (experience that is crystallized as objects of reflection, or experience that has become a mental "thing"). But these two moments reciprocate one another, such that meaning is always reconstructed and expanding, reification is always subverted by experience and hardened again in ongoing processes of reflection. Thus, learning for Wenger is always "emergent" rather than final. Wenger's dialectical approach consists

---

2. C. A. Bowers and David J. Flinders, *Responsive Teaching: An Ecological Approach to Classroom Patterns of Language, Culture, and Thought*, 199.

3. Etienne Wenger, *Communities of Practice: Learning, Meaning, and Identity.*

in sets of practices, first the practices that make up the experiences of a community, and then second-order practices in which community members reflect in constructive ways on their experiences. Wenger's model helps us to locate our notions of "catching theology in action" and "reconstructing theology in practice" as second-order practices always already in conversation with student experiences. What it means for theological thinking to be "skillful" is for these second-order practices to be well defined and well practiced in the context of seminary classrooms and then transposed by well-educated seminarians into the diverse contexts of ministry. It is the task of this essay to define these practices well.

## *The Context of the Classroom*

In this section, we focus our attention on one particular context, the seminary classroom. The classroom has its own ecological character, and paying attention to the conditions that bound the seminary classroom context suggests a model of skillful theological reflection appropriate to it. But we also want to argue that such a model points beyond the classroom, equipping students with a skill set they can import into other contexts that invite theological thinking.

Many prominent models for theological reflection in an educational context come from Clinical Pastoral Education (CPE), in which the rich events generated in clinical ministry experiences are the focus of the reflection process.[4] Whether phenomenological or process oriented, these works develop models of reflection that are explicitly and appreciably theological. The seminary classroom is, however, a different context and has different demands from those of CPE. Importantly, there is a body of course material to which reflection in the classroom is directed. Additionally, CPE facilitators are rigorously trained in a particular skill set (involving psychoanalysis and group therapy) not included in the training of most professors in seminaries or theological schools. Finally, while clinical settings certainly are important ministry contexts, existing models for ministry

---

4. See, e.g., James D. Whitehead and Evelyn Eaton Whitehead, *Method in Ministry: Theological Reflection and Christian Ministry*; John Patton, *From Ministry to Theology: Pastoral Action and Reflection*; Robert L. Kinast, *Let Ministry Teach: A Guide to Theological Reflection*.

and ministerial education developed in and for clinical settings tend to be rooted in psychoanalytic rather than ecclesial or theological practices.[5]

This is all to say that the kind of skillful theological reflection that students can learn in the seminary classroom will be different in important respects from the CPE experience. But, if done well, there will also be important similarities. Like the CPE model, skillful theological thinking in the classroom will be constructive in conversation with experience, even if experience isn't always the primary object of reflection. And, if done well, skillful thinking in the seminary classroom will be distinctly theological in the sense that it will help students do the important work of constructing theological insights as they engage course material. How does this happen?

Consider the following scenario.[6] A second-career student has been doing his field work in a large Methodist church in Atlanta. He is assigned to lead a discussion on material pertaining to the pastor's role as counselor. The material includes a selection from Henri Nouwen's well-known book *The Wounded Healer,* in which the author discusses the ways in which the pastoral role of the minister always engages her own brokenness even as she attends to the needs of others. The student leader invites discussion of that material by way of a personal story, which he shares with the class. He relates that recently

---

5. It may be observed that we are constructing a model of ministerial education in this chapter rooted in educational theory rather than ecclesial or theological practices. One challenge academic theological institutions face is that of balancing academic and ecclesial orientations. Is the governing goal to instill intellectual knowledge, or to instill attentiveness to God? To learn to think well, or to pray well? To preserve and promote disciplined forms of scientific inquiry, or disciplined forms of faithful living? Many of us may and do embrace both academic and ecclesial (and other) orientations, but it cannot really be denied that in very practical ways one or the other set of criteria tends to govern in any given context. For example, in the context of most universities a professor may earn tenure and a student may earn high marks on the basis of superior intellectual performance without regard to concerns for "faithful living"; while in the context of most churches a pastor may earn respect and advancement and a parishioner may earn honor and leadership responsibilities on the basis of faithfulness to the church without necessary regard to intellectual prowess. Since the particular context of our reflection here is the academic classroom it is appropriate that we make use of academic educational theory. Yet we are also seeking to make explicit connection to modes of reflection a pastor might use in ecclesial settings. We believe that skillful theological reflection as developed here is portable from theological classroom to ecclesial settings and is therefore appropriate for theological education for ministry.

6. This example is based on a situation that Senior encountered in a Candler Contextual Education course. It has been altered considerably in order to conceal the identity of the participants.

a parishioner with whom the student has developed a close relationship has "come out" to another pastor at the church who, from the point of view of the student, seems to be on less intimate terms with the parishioner in question. The student is clearly a very engaging person with a warm and inviting personality, and it's understandable to all in the class that one might expect anyone could confide in him. Indeed, he says, he is usually the first to find out about problems and issues that his friends are facing. But the student didn't get to be the confidant this time. He is disappointed, and he implies this somehow impugns his ability as a counselor.

Several other members of the seminar group point out that this incident along with the student's willingness to acknowledge his own feelings around it illustrates helpfully the graced shape of pastoral ministry that Nouwen is describing. "Maybe this very moment is the one in which God's grace is revealed," one suggests. All agree that the student's anecdote shows in a very practical way how we come to pastoral situations carrying along with us the cross of Christ, weighted with the pain and disappointment that we've suffered in our own journeys. Though it is not the focus of the conversation, the class also voices its support for the discussion leader's reaction to this incident. All affirm that he is indeed an important figure in this parishioner's life and that in time he will play a role in this process that is sufficient given God's grace.

There are some distinctive features of this process of theological reflection. First, the discussion is oriented around the formal course material, the Nouwen reading. A primary goal in the presentation discussion is to illuminate the insights contained in the reading. Second, with Nouwen's help and the student leader's anecdote, students begin to riff on the notion of grace, as though it were a jazz session. And when it comes time to affirm the student in this pastoral situation, those riffs come in handy.

But the focus of this seminar discussion does not turn entirely to the student and his handling of the situation. The class doesn't try to elicit whatever it is about the student's own experience that informed his reaction to the incident, nor do they dwell on the student's feelings about not being the counselor/confident in this case. These moves might be properly made in the context of CPE. Instead, here in the theological classroom, the discussion constructs theological meaning by focusing on the reported incident through the lens of the Nouwen reading as a part of the theological tradition. The assumption is that God is present and active in the incident, and that the purpose of this classroom discussion is to practice discerning and naming that presence together.

This example illustrates that skillful theological thinking in the classroom entails discerning and constructing perceptions of God's presence and action in the world in conversation with course material, class participants' views and experiences, and academic and theological traditions with awareness of institutional settings and relationships. This must be done in a way that takes experience and tradition seriously, such that the classroom itself becomes contextualized in terms of the rich experiences that students and teachers alike bring into it and the rich academic and theological traditions constituting its environment. To be sure, Nouwen can be understood well enough on a reading or two. But the dynamic interaction between Nouwen's book as the object of class discussion and the experiences of the student leader along with the insights of other course participants opened the door to new theological insight. As in this example, the goal is for students to construct new theological insights and develop a skill set useful in doing such constructive work also in other contexts.

Notice also in this example that the process of theological thinking in the classroom context is shaped by the particular members of the class with their particular backgrounds and experiences. It took a constructive process of working with Nouwen's insights in response to an actual and particular experience to stimulate a corporate process of theological reflection in which each participant contributed something rooted in their own experience.

Moreover, this process is shaped by the texts, theories, and ideas introduced by the teacher, the larger ecology of the academic institution, and the ecclesial bodies with their respective theological traditions to which the institution and class members may relate. These all must be seen as active and respected partners in the activity of contextual theological thinking in a seminary classroom. The official and explicit course material must not be treated as an immoveable object for reflection. At the same time, student experiences and perspectives must not be treated as unquestionable or inherently determinative of students' knowing. And the larger academic, ecclesial, and social environments must be acknowledged and respected (even if resisted or opposed, as in the case of pop culture as discussed in chapter 9) as shapers of thinking and knowing.

Discerning the presence and participation of God in this process is never straightforward and never definitively achieved. While such discernment is an essential theological practice, we do not equate discernment of God with knowledge of God. We suggest that theological thinking be understood as a process of constructing human knowledge about the world and ourselves in light of attempts to discern God's presence and action. Further, such construction, especially for adults in a seminary classroom, never happens *ex nihilo*. Rather, all such "construction" is always "reconstruction." There is always already theological understanding in place, guiding students' thinking and action. Skillful theological thinking must entail a process of intentional reconstruction of knowledge.

## A Contextual Process for Skillful Theological Thinking

We suggest here a model for skillful theological thinking consisting of three moments: (1) catching theology in action, (2) communal theological interpretation, and (3) practical appropriation, each discussed in turn below. This three-step approach is a theological rendering of insights that Lee Shulman has named. Shulman argues that the process of learning tends to involve three basic moves: (1) bringing what is inside of learners out (knowledge, ideas, concepts), into a public domain; (2) reconstructing that knowledge in the context of the learning community; and (3) (re)integrating the reconstructed knowledge so that it is once again part of learners' being.[7]

---

7. Lee Shulman, "Teacher Development: Roles of Domain Experience and Pedagogical Knowledge," 131ff.

## Catching Theology in Action

A primary task of the Contextual Education Reflection Seminar, or any contextualized theological classroom, is to create an environment where students' current functional theological assumptions and perceptions can be safely brought out, critically reconstructed in a learning community in ways well informed by traditional wisdom, contemporary experience, and diverse perspectives, and then reintegrated as functional understanding for guiding the students' life and ministry practices. Bringing functional theological understanding "out" is not a straightforward or easy process. Often functional theological understandings actually governing our actions are held as unconscious assumptions. To complicate matters, theology students may at times claim allegiance to formal or official theological doctrines and principles not neatly aligned with their functional theology. For example, a student serving as local pastor of a small rural church may ardently profess belief in the priesthood of all believers, but may in practice work to maintain autonomous control of worship by disallowing any lay participation — thereby exhibiting a functional theology running counter to belief in the priesthood of all believers.

Examining what one has done — examining one's actual actions and practices — is a way of discerning one's functional beliefs. Examination of actions or practices in a verbatim or case study, for example, is a way of *catching functional theology in action*. If a student can simply and honestly describe his or her actions in a verbatim of a critical ministry incident, then such actions can be examined in the classroom for the functional theology implicit in those actions. Such examination of actions and practices is, in Shulman's terms, a way of bringing outside what is inside of the learner. The case study allows similar examination in a less threatening way by focusing on actions of other actual or fictional actors in a particular incident or situation. Other pedagogical strategies for catching theology in action include examination of historical events (such as the civil rights movement) or public policies (such as legislation regarding the minimum wage).

## Theological Interpretation in the Learning Community

Once functional theological assumptions are brought out into the classroom context they may be constructively put into conversation with alternative views and assumptions. Whereas catching theology in action should involve nonjudgmental noticing, the move to interpretation entails judgment about how the assumptions uncovered relate to theological wisdom in given historical traditions and to other theological assumptions in the learning community. Teachers have primary responsibility in this phase for ensuring that theological, biblical, and ecclesial traditions are present in the thinking of the learning community. This may mean directing students' attention to relevant biblical or theological texts, or reviewing particular theological doctrines or the ways certain theological problems have been addressed by certain systematic theologians or other respected representatives of the tradition. It may also be helpful to draw varying theological assumptions out of students for comparison and contrast with the assumptions in focus.

The goal in this phase of the theological thinking process is to re-shape in the learning community previously implicit or unexamined assumptions in conscious relationship to traditional wisdom and the varying views of others. All learners have responsibility in this process for sharing their views and respecting the views of others, and for attending faithfully to valued intellectual and theological traditions. What is being explored and reconstructed in this phase are assumptions and beliefs, not actions. It is not time to say what should have been done or might be done differently another time. This is an interpretive phase of the process because it is a relational meaning-making phase. For example, the meaning of Luther's doctrine of grace may be interpreted in relation to uncovered assumptions of worthlessness. The meaning of an assumption that "more is always better" may be interpreted in relation to the Quaker or Franciscan value of simplicity. The meaning of an encounter with a homeless person may be interpreted in relation to the "blessed are the poor" passage in Matthew chapter 5. This is the heart of thinking and the gift of the academic classroom — to reflect at an intentional distance on life actions and experiences, to expose implicit assumptions, and to carefully examine intellectual ideas in a context where assumptions and ideas may be safely and skillfully reconstructed.

### Practical Theological Appropriation: Integrating Reconstructed Theological Knowledge

Authentic integration of knowledge is an ultimate learning goal, but may be beyond the scope of the classroom. We will know that students have integrated new knowledge if it is evidenced in their life actions. Skillfully constructed classroom assignments may allow us to observe some level of intellectual integration of ideas. But if we are interested in the actual practices that embody functional beliefs and practical knowledge, then we will want to see integration at the level of practice. For example, in the case above of the student local pastor who professes belief in the priesthood of all believers but disallows lay participation in worship, integration of reconstructed theological understanding ought to be evidenced in the inclusion of lay leadership in worship. Practically speaking, integration of learning happens when, and perhaps even through, the engagement in practices that embody that new learning. Therefore in some sense integration cannot be achieved in the classroom. But it can be instigated, and can be experimented with in the classroom.

The key to integration is that *the student* must pick up the pieces of a discussion, a lesson, an analyzed experience and put them together in a way that makes sense (to the student) and makes them fit with the student's existing understanding. The very personal nature of such integration makes it unlikely that a teacher will be able to tell a student how to do this. For this reason pedagogies of integration are best focused on displaying models (or examples) of integration rather than theories, explanations, or instructions.

Pedagogical processes such as those involving role play, drama, bodily movement, and thought experiments may create possibilities for modeling and "enacting" integration in the classroom. Similarly, although more cerebrally, engagement with fictional or nonfictional narratives may also constitute integrated life-enactments of certain ideas or experiences, for example in short stories, novels, biographies, or movies.

## *Conclusion*

We have suggested a way of understanding skillful theological think-ing as a dimension of contextual theological education that entails processes of bringing out what is inside of students, so that this may be critically reconstructed in the learning community (in relation to the perspectives of others and in reference to Scripture, tradition, rea-son, and experience), and then reintegrated by students such that their ways of thinking and being are changed. We have sought to describe a model for skillful theological thinking and a means for creating pos-sibilities for reconstructing functional theology in practice. We have focused on the context of the seminary classroom.

But we seek to point beyond the classroom and also back to it at the same time. That is, the models for theological thinking deployed in other contexts — in clinical pastoral and parish contexts, say, or in seminary courses in theological ethics or systematic theology — bear "family resemblances," to use Wittgenstein's term, to the classroom context as we've imagined it here, and it is on this basis that our model speaks to those contexts. All of these construct knowledge in communities (of the past, present, and future) and in conversation with Scripture, tradition, reason, and experience. Our model recom-mends an intentional and sustained conversation between experience and the resources of academic reflection that bears fruit immediately in the classroom and sows the seeds for important developments beyond it. It also pushes traditional seminary pedagogy to regard students' experiences in ministry and in general as important sources of theological knowledge to be mined in the classroom. Finally, our approach prepares students for fruitful theological thinking along the many paths of ministry.

# Chapter 4

# Pedagogical Lessons from Students in Ecclesial Contexts

*P. Alice Rogers and Robert Winstead*

In many seminaries, the students enrolled often are divided into two categories: those serving churches part time while they fulfill the academic requirements for ordination (i.e., student pastors) and those whose principal focus is the academic degree. Such oversimplification is not intentional; it naturally occurs as faculty and administration differentiate between two primary categories of students who have traditionally made up the student body of most seminaries. Because this distinction is often made, it follows that judgments and comparisons between these two categories are also observed. For instance, questions concerning academic performance, community involvement, and preparedness for parish ministry are often discussed in light of these two categories. Are student pastors more prepared for parish ministry? Are the students who live on or near campus more engaged in their academic studies? Does one category of students get more out of their seminary education than the other? Such questions generate lively discussions concerning which category benefits the most from (and is most beneficial to) theological education. For the faculty member who desires the undivided attention of students engaged in theological education, the ideal student would be one whose attention is not divided between academic studies and ministerial responsibilities of a parish. Such divided attention is the basis of many frustrations for both the student and the teacher. And yet students serving in ecclesial contexts bring unique gifts and opportunities to the classroom. In fact, student pastors, by their very presence in the classroom, make contributions to theological education that may, in fact, enhance pedagogical techniques from which all students might benefit.

As we began to consider the ways in which student pastors may be a gift to theological education, we sent out a very simple questionnaire to all full-time faculty members at Candler School of Theology and to all of the students serving churches as student pastors. The questions were quite simple. The students were asked:

1. What is helpful or positive about being a student pastor while attending seminary?

2. What are the challenges or difficulties in serving a church while attending seminary?

3. In your experience, what differences do you see in students who serve as student pastors and nonstudent pastors?

The faculty was asked very similar questions:

1. What is helpful or positive about teaching students who are serving churches while attending seminary?

2. What are the challenges or difficulties in teaching students who are serving churches while attending seminary?

3. In your experience, what differences do you see in students who serve as student pastors and nonstudent pastors?

The responses helped articulate:

1. the frustrations and tensions that arise from both being and teaching this category of student;

2. the important contributions student pastors make to theological education; and

3. how these contributions can inform pedagogies for the contextualizing of theological education.

Because Candler School of Theology is one of the thirteen theological schools of the United Methodist Church, the category of student pastor has a long history with Candler. From its earliest days, students who have been licensed to preach in the Methodist Church have had the opportunity to serve small membership churches while they attend seminary. However, during the first half of the twentieth century (and Candler's first half century as an institution) the student body at Candler was entirely male and white and predominantly young. Most were supported in their studies by their families and home churches. Following World War II, as veterans returned to studies, the average age of the student body rose slightly. In the 1960s enrollment was opened to African Americans, and in the 1970s women began to enroll in significant numbers. During this time the student body became increasingly diverse and the numbers of students serving full or part time as student local pastors grew. When students serving local churches became the majority of students enrolled at Candler in the mid-1970s, the Teaching Parish Program was instituted in an effort to provide supervision for these students serving in ecclesial contexts. As the program developed, it embraced two additional purposes, the integration of experiential and theoretical learnings and the provision of a support structure for these student pastors.

The model embraced by the Teaching Parish Program to provide this supervision, integration, and support involves students meeting in small groups led by teaching supervisors, who are ordained elders in the United Methodist Church. These groups are set up to meet in geographically coordinated areas so that students do not have to commute to the Emory campus for this particular class, and so that they will have the opportunity to be in conversation with other student pastors serving in their geographic area. Candler School of Theology has maintained this long history of engagement with student pastors; and yet the relationship between the academy and those serving in such contexts has not always been ideal, primarily because of the fragmented, overextended lives student pastors traditionally have led.

Historically, student pastors have experienced a unique engagement with the seminary as they divide their time between the church, the academy, their families, and commuting. The variety of roles they balance, more often than not, has created tension between their academic studies and their pastoral leadership as well as tension for faculty who find it frustrating to teach students whose attention is so divided. As indicated in the responses to the questionnaire, that tension arises from a variety of sources.

The primary source of tension identified in the responses was stated simply as "time." To the question, "What are the challenges and difficulties in serving a church while attending seminary?" the respondents immediately stated, "Time," "Managing time," "Prioritizing time between family, school, and church." One wrote in frustration, "There are only twenty-four hours in a day!" These immediate responses were followed by litanies of all the responsibilities and duties that must take place during those twenty-four hours: commuting long distances to and from their parishes, completing academic assignments, taking care of families, preparing for Sunday worship services, fulfilling pastoral care responsibilities, and, at some point, actually sleeping. Faculty voiced similar concerns for this category of student pastors: "These students are often very pressed for time"; "too many students who are serving churches suffer from being seriously overworked"; "it is rare in my experience that a student local pastor is not severely overextended"; "their plate overflows." While time was stated as the culprit of tension and frustration, in reality, it is the large number of tasks and obligations that a student pastor is expected to meet in the twenty-four hours allotted to each day.

Another source of tension, which is directly related to this over-extension and the difficulty of balancing a myriad of responsibilities, is mediocre academic performance. This source of tension was identified by both faculty and student pastors. A first year student pastor, who had been a straight A student in undergraduate school, bemoaned the fact that he simply did not have the time to produce the quality work of which he was capable and confessed that this diminished performance affected his self-esteem. Another student exclaimed, "It is so stressful when an emergency in your church occurs, and you have to drive a hundred or two hundred miles that evening and be back the next morning for a test." Likewise, faculty complained that "the student pastors' schedules are crazy, and they are all too often bound to be the 'pastor' first and the student second"; and "because they are stretched so thin, they sometimes get by with the minimum effort"; and "because they are overextended, they miss the joy of attending seminary and do just enough to get by." As these

tensions and frustrations escalate, it often leads to comments like this
one voiced by a faculty member: "If I had my way, no student would
serve a church beyond the seminary requirements."

And yet in spite of the challenges that face both student pastors and
faculty as they engage in the classroom, there are many benefits and
opportunities to be gained from the student pastors' experience of
serving in ecclesial contexts. Because many seminaries in this twenty-
first century have identified as their mission the education of persons
for effective ministry in the church and in the world, seminary students who are employed as pastors in ecclesial settings bring diverse
and valuable resources into the academic life of the seminary. These
student pastors enhance the mission of the seminary by fostering an
approach to learning that constantly seeks to integrate the parish and
the academy.

First of all, contextual questions and issues are always at the forefront for the student pastor. Because they live, breathe, eat, and sleep
in the very contexts about which they study, the real world human
condition is by default a part of the pedagogical context. To the
question, "What is helpful about teaching students who are serving
churches while attending seminary?" one professor focused on this
contribution: "They bring experiences from the parish to the classroom and those experiences inform the kinds of questions they ask."
And, the same faculty member who exclaimed that no student should
serve a church beyond the limited seminary requirements confessed
that "student pastors bring up 'real life experiences' almost as case
studies of issues we are discussing in class." Such "real life experiences" are witnessed across the curriculum. In Religious Education,
a student pastor who is debating with a Sunday school superinten-
dent over Sunday school material brings immediate questions to the
classroom of how to theologically critique curriculum; as they study
issues of baptism in church history, student pastors often are encountering similar debates in their own churches; in Pastoral Care, student
pastors listen intently knowing that when they drive home that night,
they may be called to visit a family experiencing a crisis; they bring
to Christian ethics the situations facing individuals with whom they
have visited and prayed. The contexts of the ecclesial settings quite

naturally lend themselves to current experiences and issues being discussed theoretically in the classroom. And because student pastors embody what they experience in their parishes as they live in those contexts day in and day out, they necessarily bring those experiences to the academy.

Not only do student pastors bring relevant, current experience into the classroom, but there are immediate opportunities for integration between what they are learning theoretically with what they are experiencing practically. Student pastors quickly acknowledge the advantages of living in both the church and the academy: "I listen in more productive ways"; "I can immediately integrate learnings from seminary into the parish"; "I also have access to people in seminary who can help me work through 'parish opportunities' as they come up — a resource I will never have again." Faculty agree that the parish is the natural setting for immediate application of theory and praxis: "Student pastors are able to test new information in the crucible of their local church"; "they are on the job so they can try things out and begin to learn the skills of 'translation' "; "material taught is immediately useful." One professor related a story that ideally illustrates this gift: "I recall one particularly good student who found in the work of one of the theologians we had read a vision that enabled him to deal with an unusually conservative congregation that had been prepared to be suspicious of him. He discovered in that theologian's view of the nature of language an approach that helped him listen to what was beneath the words that his parishioners used and to see some of the underlying issues in them. It helped him accept them (even though his vision of the church was far different from theirs) and it helped them accept him (because they found that he wasn't out to subvert their faith)." This dynamic created by living in both the academy and the parish offers opportunities for immediate integration, for not only will the student bring the questions of the parish into the classroom, but the theories taught may be used to analyze and understand the issues of the parish.

Another related benefit of the student pastor's presence in the classroom is the development of theological reflection in the context of the hurts and hopes of the world. Quality theological inquiry requires a careful attentiveness to mercy and justice as applied to persons' lives.

The student pastor often asks, "How can what I'm learning make a difference in the world?" The stimulation of the parish context enables the student pastor to consider and apply theological truths to the struggles inherent in the human condition and find creative ways to serve as both theologian and pastor. Hence, if the mission of the academy includes the preparation of leaders to participate in the ministries of justice and reconciliation, then that grounding is strengthened by the student pastor living and working in community with lay persons. Often it is the lay person who will ask the difficult questions, raise the difficult issues, and refuse to take easy answers. The student pastor deals with the real issues of parishioners' lives and so learns to reflect critically and constructively on theology in context, the connection between the Christian faith and the real world. Other students benefit when the student pastor shares this connection in the academic setting, enhancing and deepening the classroom experience.

While student pastors move between the parish and the academy, bringing the practical to the theoretical and translating the theoretical to practical living, they also bring opportunities for building connective partnerships between the seminary and the parish (which also has pedagogical implications). One of those opportunities involves the maintenance of communication between denominational conferences/judicatories and the academy. It is a constant challenge to align seminary education with judicatory requirements, and the presence of student pastors enables those requirements to maintain a place of high visibility and priority for the academy since these students are preparing for ordination. Another opportunity for connection includes the means for continuous communication and conversation between the local church and the seminary. As long as student pastors bring the parish experience into the classroom, the temptation for faculty to use the parish as just an object of study is lessened. The relevance of the parish to the academy and conversely, the academy to the parish, is maintained through the student pastor. And finally, since studies show that only about 50 percent of seminary students enter local church ministry, opportunities exist for conversation on how non-profit, chaplaincy, counseling, and other ministry occupations beyond the local church connect and interrelate with local church ministries.

Because student pastors serve in ecclesial contexts and are able, therefore, to bring a variety of experiences to the classroom, their very presence can inform pedagogies that seek to contextualize theological education by providing checks to both theory and practice, encouraging faculty to create integrative assignments, and offering a means to evaluate the connection between church and academy.

One of the primary ways in which the presence and experience of student pastors living in the day-to-day life of the local church can inform pedagogy concerns the opportunities by which faculty can evaluate their own theory. For instance, many professors use case studies they have prepared or collected to reflect on theory and to provide examples of how theory can be observed in context. A problem inherent in this technique is the risk that only case studies that support the theory professed will be chosen. Case studies can easily be used to manipulate theory and advance only one line of thinking and research. However, if a professor encourages those serving in ecclesial contexts to bring current case studies to class, such studies can richly inform, critique, or reinforce the theory being taught.

In addition, by utilizing students' immediate experience, faculty members are able to explore theory on a much deeper and richer level with their class. One such example involved a student listening to a lecture on creating the correct acoustics for a sanctuary. Since very poor acoustics were a concern of her parish, she listened carefully; however, when the lecturer declared that any carpet in the sanctuary should simply be ripped out, she had immediate concerns. The student knew that in her small, rural church, Miss Sadie had given the sanctuary carpet in memory of her brother who had committed suicide on Christmas Day years before. She knew beyond a shadow of a doubt (and from the experience of trying to move the baptismal font from a closet to the front of the sanctuary) that while the carpet was worn and stained and did indeed hinder the acoustics of the worship space, it would take much pastoral care, creative administrative skill, and intentional relationship building for the suggestion to remove or change the carpet to be approached, much less implemented. While the theory may have been sound and absolutely correct, the immediate, contextual experience of the student serving in the local church enabled the topic to be discussed from the perspective of praxis, rather than theory alone. A deeper, richer, more integrative discussion ensued as current, immediate experience engaged theoretical learning.

Such pedagogy requires that both student and teacher be open to continuous learning. The professor cannot rigidly defend theory or dismiss experience that challenges theory, nor can the student insist that all personal experience is an adequate critique of theory or the final standard by which theory is judged. Yet if student and teacher are committed to the constant and dynamic dialogue that can and should exist between the church and the academy as real life experience and theory are encountered in context, faculty have the unique opportunity constantly to engage the theories they study, and curriculum becomes informed and formed as the dialog between theory and practice continues.

Another way in which the presence of student pastors can inform pedagogy is by the fact that their presence encourages faculty to create assignments that purposively integrate theory with praxis. Faculty who teach in praxis disciplines intentionally focus on the practical aspects of theological education, and their assignments quite naturally lend themselves to such integration; however, those who teach in non-praxis disciplines can creatively address these same practical issues. For example, discussions concerning issues such as theodicy, Christian ethics, sacramental theology, biblical interpretation, and church history can easily be addressed from the perspective of what is happening currently in the context of a local church. On any given day, a student pastor may be approached by a parishioner asking questions that require the application of biblical interpretation principles. An assignment in which the student must parse a conversation in terms of how those principles were employed contextualizes the theory taught. Assignments that require theological concepts be translated to a Wednesday morning women's Bible study group requires that the theoretical discussions of the classroom be applied to the contexts in which ministry takes place. As experience is brought to the classroom and as theory is applied in context, learning becomes dynamic and connective, flowing between the classroom and context. One setting is not held as superior to the other as the church and academy inform one another. In fact, such pedagogy advances the practice many theological educators seek to instill in their students, the ability to think well theologically about and within real contexts. Hence, the very presence of student pastors in the classroom provides opportunities for faculty to create contextualized assignments.

Such integrative assignments also enable seminary faculty to maintain a connective check on their research, study, and teaching. That is, faculty can evaluate the effectiveness of integrative, dynamic learning by asking the question, "Does my pedagogy widen or close the gap between the church and the academy?" The attendance of those serving in ecclesial contexts allows this question to maintain a prominent place in the evaluative process, for their presence enables faculty to maintain open, honest, and candid conversations about that connection. They are able to ask, "How is this (fact, theory, hypothesis, supposition) confirmed or substantiated in your local church?" or "Would this (fact, theory, hypothesis, supposition) be challenged or disputed in your local church?" or "Does this (fact, theory, hypothesis, supposition) even matter in your local church, and if not, why?" When such connective questions are considered seriously, the connection between the church and the academy is strengthened.

As faculty work intentionally to make the connections between praxis and theory and between the church and the academy, the classroom itself can become the place where connections are made for students who experience much fragmentation as they balance a variety of responsibilities. While two categories of students were identified at the beginning of this chapter, in reality, students could be divided into numerous categories. In any given seminary classroom, students will consist of those who attend seminary full time, those who have a part-time position on a church staff, those who serve small membership churches as the sole pastor, those who work in secular jobs on a part-time or full-time basis, those who have extensive family responsibilities, or are single, etc. Students may range in age from twenty-three to sixty-five and represent a wide diversity of denominations, cultures, races, theological beliefs, etc. Instead of two categories of students, the current reality finds classrooms filled with students that could be divided into a multitude of categories.

As a result, faculty members are faced with the challenge of teaching students whose attention is divided not just between the parish and the academy, but whose attention is divided in hundreds of ways. Yet if faculty take into account the pedagogical lessons discerned from teaching students serving in ecclesial contexts, as considered in this chapter, instead of the classroom being one more experience of fragmentation and disconnection for students, it becomes the place where wholeness and connection are modeled. By enabling all students to reflect on the diverse contexts in which they live, work, and play, and seeking ways to create a dynamic relationship between the classroom and students' everyday contexts, such intentional pedagogical connection enables theological education to promote wholeness.

In summary, while theological educators may yearn for students who are able to give their undivided attention to their studies within the academy, the pedagogical lessons of relevance, integration, pastoral awareness, and academy/parish connection provided by the presence of student pastors in the classroom are extraordinarily helpful in addressing the growing challenges of teaching an ever increasingly diverse student body whose fragmented lives cause them to be more engaged with responsibilities outside of the academy than within.

# Chapter 5

# Black Theology and Pedagogy
### *Noel Leo Erskine*

This essay examines the emergence of black theology as a discipline within the academy and investigates how black theology may serve as a resource for contextual theological teaching and learning. The impetus for the construction and articulation of this theology was the exclusion of black people by white religionists. Black theologians were careful not to adopt the exclusionary approach of white religionists in relation to white men but included them both in the exposition and analysis of its major themes and arguments. I find it instructive for pedagogy in classroom and church that black theologians refused to pattern God-talk from the white model of exclusion but have insisted instead that if theology is to be in the service of creating and sustaining a compassionate and diverse community, then the stranger must be embraced both in the academy and church. Yet in the first decade of its development all the theologians were men, and it did not occur to these black male theologians that women, particularly black women, were excluded.

Taking my cue from black theologians' successes and shortcomings I would like to examine what it means in the classroom to include the stranger, the person of a different race, ethnicity, religion, culture, or sex. While including the (white) stranger black theologians excluded women of the same race, ethnicity, religion, and history. While the outsider from another race, ethnicity, and culture was included the insider from the same race, ethnicity, and culture was excluded. One reason for the exclusion of black women by black theologians had to do with the notion of sameness. Because black women were of the same race, culture, and in many cases religion they were ignored as black theologians failed to recognize that sameness does not mean identicalness. While they saw white men as different and construed difference in terms of unknowability, they failed to see difference in black women in terms of transcendence. I would like to investigate to what extent black theologians in making peace with the immanence that confronted them in black women overlooked issues of transcendence. We must inquire, What does it mean to affirm the transcendence of the person of the same race, ethnicity, culture, and religion? How may we discover that transcendence is hidden in immanence?

Other themes to be explored have to do with continuities between the classroom and the black church. Is the space created in the classroom transgressive space in which all are permitted to risk their own voice and identity, as is often the case in the black church? Should good teaching and learning include testimonies, stories of resistance and adventure? James Cone in his important book *Risks of Faith* and bell hooks in *Teaching to Transgress* provide important help in this discussion.[1] Also of first importance is the article by black theologian J. Deotis Roberts "Liberating Theological Education: Can Our Seminaries Be Saved"?[2] in which he contends that in theological education we must do more than ask about the continuities between church and classroom; we must also ask about the continuities between the cries of the oppressed in our societies and the classroom. Because the cry that exudes from the oppressed is the cry for liberation, according to Roberts we must inquire if education is for liberation and reconciliation. In February 1983 when this article by Roberts was published, he did not identify the subservient place of black women in church and academy as needing liberation. This is especially poignant since he wrote as president of the Interdenominational Theological Center in Atlanta. Roberts called attention to the need in the theological school and church to ground pedagogy in black culture and history and resist the urge to be anti-intellectual as black people accept themselves as made in the image of God. He frames the issue for us:

---

1. James Cone, *Risks of Faith: The Emergence of a Black Theology of Liberation, 1968–1998;* bell hooks, *Teaching to Transgress: Education as the Practice of Freedom.*

2. J. Deotis Roberts, "Liberating Theological Education: Can Our Seminaries Be Saved?" 98, 113–16.

When Blacks excavate their African roots, they participate in a holistic view of reality. When we are at home with ourselves and our culture, and not trying to be like somebody else, we are holistic in thought and faith. We are never liberated until we make this discovery. What this means is that we Blacks have a real contribution to make to theology and the Christian movement — if we can be set free. Thus, the first item on our agenda may be the psychological freedom to think and believe out of our own culture and history.[3]

Roberts is quite helpful as a black theologian in giving us a feel for the central questions on the agenda of black theologians in the second decade of black theology's advent as an academic discipline, and a sense of the contribution black theology could make in the classroom. According to Roberts black theology is significant for pedagogy because black theology offers pedagogy a holistic world-view in its affirmation of the unity of body and soul, secular and sacred, piety and activism. Further, black theology inspires pedagogy in that it points to the black community's "ability to transmute personal and group suffering into moral victory.... The tendency to surround each other with love and community in tough times is to be cherished."[4]

Roberts reminds us that theological education seen within the prism of liberation and reconciliation must be priestly and prophetic. It must be priestly as it seeks to conserve values of self-love and renounce the penchant for imitation. Theological education must also be prophetic as it places values of social justice and human worth at the center of the curriculum and life together in the seminary community.

Black seminarians at predominantly White seminaries are asking to be recognized as persons of worth. They are calling for attention to curriculum offerings more in keeping with their future ministry.... There is a worsening of the situation for Blacks at White seminaries as resources decline. Since concern for the

---

3. Ibid., 115.
4. Ibid., 116.

Black agenda was never central to most seminaries, the shortage of funds seems to be the answer to the prayers of those who would maintain the status quo on race relations.[5]

Black theologians during the first two decades of the development of black theology mirrored the position of Roberts. The main difference was a matter of emphasis and methodology, not a fundamental shift in substance or focus. For example, Cecil Wayne Cone's *The Identity Crisis in Black Theology* was a theological quarrel with his brother, James Cone, in which he challenged his brother to give priority to black religion in the articulation of black theology. But there was no quarrel concerning the common task at hand; they were agreed that the central theological problem was racism. And part of what this meant was they would engage white theologians in the academy and church as they challenged structures of oppression that were organized against the human flourishing of oppressed people.

## Pedagogy and the Black Community

Black theologians were agreed that the first truth was truth about the black community, the recounting of their stories and the affirmation of their heritage. J. Deotis Roberts would join the quarrel with James Cone as to whether or not the hermeneutical key was liberation or reconciliation, but they were agreed that the problem was racism. To identify the problem was to begin to press for liberation and reconciliation. They sought to free their people with truth as they engaged those within church and academy who would compromise their humanity. Although the problem as black theologians stated it had to do with white theologians within the academy and church who rendered black people invisible, they refused to pattern their approach to pedagogy and God-talk after the method of exclusion adopted and embraced by white academicians and theologians within the church. Black theologians observed that if theology would be in the service of pedagogy in church and academy as it sought to fashion a compassionate and diverse community, then the neighbor as stranger and critic had to be embraced.

---

5. Ibid.

Because black theology is Christian theology and affirms the church as the home of theology, it begins to make sense that with the influence of the black church in the background and quite often in the foreground, the church's reference to the biblical injunction to be hospitable to strangers, Hebrews 13:1–2, would be taken seriously. James Cone in his *God of the Oppressed* informs us that he was licensed to preach at age sixteen. This invitation to be hospitable to strangers would have been part of the ethos in the African Methodist Church in which he was reared in Bearden, Arkansas. There was always an element of fear in the black church that God would treat us the way we treated strangers. There was no attempt in the black church to practice reverse discrimination, and no one exemplifies this better than Martin Luther King Jr. Cone in his important book *Martin and Malcolm and America: A Dream or a Nightmare* points to the role of the civil rights movement in the United States under the leadership of King as indispensable for the visioning and articulation of black theology. Martin Luther King Jr. indicates that the black church's understanding of what it means to be human in church as in the academy is an outgrowth of their understanding of who God is.

Because God is a God of Love who is generous to all God's children and does not privilege one group of children over another, it means that all God's children have virtue and inherent worth, even if some of God's children advocate segregation and racism. King would insist that every human being by virtue of being human has inherent worth, and no person, society, or culture has the right to deny his or her dignity. The bottom line for King was that racism was a sin against God. Love for God meant working to dismantle the very fabric of racism. But in spite of the human condition soiled by racism every human being may claim respect because God loves him or her. "The worth of an individual does not lie in the measure of his intellect, racial origin, or social position. Human worth lies in relatedness to God. An individual has value because he has value to God."[6] Because God's love is the basis of the worth of human beings, it means that all

---

6. Martin Luther King Jr., "The Ethical Demands for Integration," in *A Testament of Hope: The Essential Writings of Martin Luther King, Jr.*, 122.

persons are of equal worth. There is no theological or biblical basis for regarding white people as superior to black people. King echoes the black church's perspective:

> Our Hebraic-Christian tradition refers to this inherent dignity of man in the biblical term the image of God. This innate worth referred to in the phrase the image of God is universally shared in equal portions by all men. There is no graded scale of essential worth: there is no divine right of one race which differs from the divine right of another. Every human being has etched in his personality the indelible stamp of the creator[7]

It is important to note that Cone, like his mentor King, could insist on a relationship of love for the critic and neighbor who sought to render black people invisible and in some instances to destroy black people. For both King and Cone there was an indissoluble relationship between love and justice. King, while learning this in the black church, gave it theological exposition and analysis in his dissertation for Boston University on the thought of Henry Nelson Wieman and Paul Tillich. From Tillich King learned that any responsible attempt to practice love in church, society, or the academy has to take seriously the interrelatedness of love, power, and justice. King would often remind his hearers that love without power is anemic and power without love is calculated.

King was forced to engage this analysis because of the leaders of the Student Non-Violent Coordinating Committee (SNCC), who pointed out to King that in his constant plea for black people to confront white brutality with nonviolent resistance, to turn the other cheek, he was calling on black people to love white people without demanding that black people practice justice towards themselves in learning to love themselves. The students contended that there was nothing that hurt oppressed people as too much love for others, especially when the intent of others was to destroy them. This was an important lesson for King and black theologians: the danger of always loving self last often meant not at all, as one never got around to finding time or space to love self. The students taught King and Cone that love as it

---

7. Ibid., 118–19.

engages power must insist on justice. Both King and Cone understood justice as the essence of love. But the mistake that both King and Cone made was seeing justice only in terms of the analysis of the structures of alienation and oppression.

Although intellectually King understood, and Cone reminds us, that an examination of relations of love, power, and justice must begin with justice, these theologians did not practice love and accord justice to women who were close at hand. This was why in the case of King women were often not affirmed in leadership positions in the running of the civil rights movement. Because women were the most vulnerable they were often excluded when opportunities for leadership in the movement presented themselves, and if given an opportunity to lead, they were often not affirmed. It stands to reason then that there were no women among black theologians in the first few decades of the development of black theology. Further, it should not surprise us that the names of women who were active in the civil rights movement do not come to mind as readily as the names of men who identified with Martin Luther King Jr. Most students of the civil rights movement are familiar with the names of Jessie Jackson, Ralph David Abernathy, John Lewis, Andrew Young, C. T. Vivian, and James Lawson. But if asked to name women who were identified with the movement they stop at Coretta Scott King, the wife of the slain civil rights leader.

There is a sense in which women were rendered invisible in the movement. Not that they were not contributors, because Rosa Parks started the trail that led to the movement. As someone has said, "She sat down so that Martin Luther King Jr. could stand up." Further, it was the Women's Political Council at Alabama State College, led by Jo Ann Robinson, that got the leaflets out to advertise the bus boycott. Besides, both the jails and freedom rides were crowded with women. Women who had leadership roles in the movement were Dorothy Cotton, the director of the Citizenship Education Program (CEP); Septima Clark, who was director of the workshops of CEP; and Ella Baker, who organized the Southern Christian Leadership Conference (SCLC) and served as acting director for a short while. Commenting on Baker's tenure as acting director, Cone states:

Although she served as its "acting director," most of the male preachers were uneasy with her presence because she did not exhibit the "right attitude" [read "submissiveness"?] which they expected from women, an expectation no doubt shaped by the role of women in their churches. Ella Baker's tenure with SCLC was relatively brief (though longer than she expected), largely because of her conflicts with King and others regarding their attitude toward women and their leadership style built around the charisma of one person — Martin Luther King, Jr. Baker preferred the group-centered leadership developed by SNCC, whose founding she initiated.[8]

Both King and Cone because of their first commitment to analysis of structures of domination and oppression were able to make room for the stranger, the person of a different race, ethnicity, and class as love was translated as truth confronting power and justice was viewed as an analysis of structures of oppression. In embracing the stranger, the person of a different race, they neglected the most vulnerable among them: the black woman. This is surprising because both black theology as articulated by Cone, and certainly by J. Deotis Roberts, and King's articulation of the Beloved Community have the openness that provides for the inclusion of women. The exclusion of women points to the gap between theory and practice, oughtness and isness.

## *Black and Christian*

One of the challenges that faces black theology at this point of our discussion as theology seeks to engage pedagogy is to ask in what way is black theology Christian theology, and further what is the appropriate response of black theology to racism in church and academy. The first question regarding the status of black theology in relation to Christian theology becomes important as we recall that in the articulation of black theology, black power played a central role. Issues of self-determination and self-acceptance were crucial as lessons from black history and black culture sought to illuminate the ethical response of black people to a racist environment that was marginalizing

---

8. James Cone, *Martin and Malcolm and America: A Dream or a Nightmare*, 278.

and rendering them invisible. Black people had to live with a past and present reality in which many white people denied their existence as children of God. This is certainly one reason why the majority of black Christians are outside the white church, and it became important for the black community to found and establish black institutions of worship and higher learning. Martin Luther King Jr. reminded us that 11:00 a.m. on Sundays is the most segregated hour in America as black and white congregations gathered for worship. For better or for worse, we are separated. The turn of black church/black theology to black power was to identify the root cause of the problem as racism.

As black theology engages pedagogy we must acknowledge that the primordial springs that nurture and nourish black existence are different from those of white people. Black theology reminds us of the difference in the long history of suffering in the U.S. American South that shaped the soul of black people. As W. E. B. Du Bois taught us, to be black in America is to be African and American at the same time. Black theology as it engages pedagogy must deal with this twoness. To be black in America is to live in the tension between freedom and bondage. The overcoming of the many forms of bondage that afflict the black community is not found in sacrificial love that insists on loving self last. The truth is that this has always been part of our problem because last means never finding time or the courage to love self. Black theology coupled with black power instructs black people to accept their uniqueness. As J. Deotis Roberts admonished us earlier the challenge is the freedom not to imitate white values and the white way of life as the way forward.

This means that black theology seeks to become Christian theology on two fronts. On the one hand it insists on the primacy of community. It is not enough for the response to racism to be private and personal, but it issues forth out of the life of the black community. Echoing John Mbiti in *African Religions and Philosophy* the response from within the church and academy should be "I am because we are. It is because we are that I am." To be human is to be in community. The second challenge as black theology seeks to become Christian theology is that black theology does not merely seek to interpret black existence but to transform institutional life in such a way that the black community becomes a window through which other peoples can get a glimpse of what it looks like to become more like Christ. It is precisely at this point that black theology instructs pedagogy in terms of its Christian responsibility in a racist school and a racist church.

As black theology informs pedagogy, the challenge facing blacks in the classroom and in the church is how to be black and Christian at the same time. A part of what this means is that loyalty to Christ does not obviate loyalty to one's cultural and historical legacy. The black Christian acknowledges the legacy of slavery and Jim Crow-ism, the history of racial segregation and oppression in America. The struggle in these multiple contexts is for liberation and reconciliation that simultaneously accept where black people are and chart the way forward. The way forward is to dream of transformation in church and classroom. It is in this context that blacks are allowed and given the right to speak their own words, to name their own reality and to dream new dreams.

## *Learning from the Stranger*

There is a sense in which black theology's turn to the stranger was a turn towards dreams of reconciliation and eschatological hope — hope for wholeness and healing in race relations. In any case, a look at Cone's *Black Theology and Black Power* reveals black theology's commitment to white ways of talking about God, humanity, and the world. Cone engages white thinkers as diverse as Emil Brunner, Rudolf Bultmann, Dietrich Bonhoeffer, Günther Bornkamm, Billy Graham, Karl Jasper, Søren Kierkegaard, and Richard Niebuhr, to name a few. Cone informs the reader that he was introduced to white thinkers in seminary and graduate school and wrote his dissertation on Karl Barth's anthropology. What is instructive in Cone's turn to white thinkers is a willingness to be in conversation with the critic and stranger in spite of the white stranger's commitment to humiliate and to render black people invisible. Cone puts it this way:

> When I graduated with a bachelor of arts degree from Philan-
> der Smith and was accepted at Garrett Theological Seminary in

Evanston, Illinois (now Garrett-Evangelical), I was a little naïve, for I was sure that things would be different. I had internalized the myth that Blacks were treated equally "up north," but that myth was demolished for me in less than one day in Evanston and Garrett. Although racism at Garrett and in Evanston was not as obvious as in Arkansas, I believe that it was much more vicious, especially in terms of the structural brutality inflicted upon Black dignity and self-confidence. I almost did not survive past my first quarter at Garrett, making all C's from professors who told me that I deserved less. This was a common experience for the few Blacks allowed to matriculate at Garrett during the late 1950's and early '60's.[9]

This was the experience of many black persons who dared to darken the academic halls of white institutions of higher learning also in the 1970s and early 1980s throughout the United States. This was one reason for the formation of black caucuses in many white institutions throughout the United States. Black caucuses provided black sacred space where black people did not have to struggle against the white myth of being inferior but were free to allow black history and culture to illuminate their being together in community and their discourse about what it means to be human in an environment in which black dignity and black self-respect are constantly under attack. It is also of interest to note that in 1970, black professors of religion throughout the United States formed the Society for the Study of Black Religion, which was aimed at providing black sacred space for theological discourse. The fact that this society is still in existence and numbers over one hundred colleagues calls attention to the need for a creative context in the academy where black people will be taken seriously as they allow their history and culture and the black religious experience to illuminate theological discourse. Perhaps Cone's turn to white colleagues in the academy is one way of acknowledging the need for the creation of sacred space where respect and dignity are accorded all participants and black people and others do not have to fear "receiving all Cs."

---

9. James Cone, "The Gospel and the Liberation of the Poor," 162–66.

It is to the credit of black theologians that the door has always been cracked for communication and dialog with the person of a different race. In spite of the history of oppression, Cone has always insisted that the "conversation matters," that there is much to learn from the stranger. Cone seems to suggest that strangers are our neighbors and that God has given us neighbors for us to respect, to safeguard their dignity, and to learn from them. This is an important key as black theology informs pedagogy and seeks to create black sacred space for conversation informed by dignity and respect. While I am not sure black theology as articulated by Cone is able to go all the way as instructed by Leviticus 19:33–34, it is quite clear in its embrace of the stranger that it is headed in the right direction.

> When a stranger resides with you in your land, you shall not do him wrong. The stranger who resides with you shall be to you as the native among you, and you shall love him as yourself; for you were aliens in the land of Egypt: I am the Lord your God. (NASB)

What lessons are there in this text that may guide us in the embrace of the stranger? Are we able to honor the biblical injunction to love the stranger as we love self?

It is precisely at this point that the sacrament of hospitality becomes crucial for pedagogical practices. What would the practice of love for self and neighbor look like in the classroom? The biblical injunction seeks to take us further than black theology is able. It seeks to engage in emancipatory pedagogy as the biblical text encourages us to set goals and engage in practices that foster a liberating consciousness. Frederick Douglass said, "We should not expect crops without tilling the soil." We should not expect members of a class to learn to love self and neighbor without participating in the telling of their own stories. It stands as a pedagogical maxim that we cannot free ourselves with practices that are anchored in the narrative of others. As members of a class we must be willing to place our stories in conversation with others.

Listening to strangers is at the same time a willingness to take ourselves seriously. Students often ask concerning contexts in which they feel devalued: "How should I respond in a class that defines me as C?" The student as stranger identifies the tension between what she knows she is essentially and the way her context portrays her. The way forward is love for self, which includes the practice of justice toward self. This means an attitude of affirmation and a struggle to explode the myths that marginalize and circumscribe one as a member of a class. Students should be encouraged not to respond in the way they are defined. The student has to rebel, the student has to "talk back." The other must be encountered as a person. This is part of what it means to teach and learn after the advent of black theology.

## Black Theology and the Black Woman

While black theology took pains in addressing the stranger, it overlooked the black woman as friend, mother, and sister who was close at hand. Cone in a confessional note places the issue before us:

> Although Black women represent more than one-half of the population in the Black community and 75 percent in the Black Church, their experience has not been visibly present in the development of Black Theology. For the most part, Black male theologians have remained conspicuously silent on feminist theology generally and Black women in particular. We have spoken of the Black religious experience as if it consisted only of our male experience with no distinctive contribution from Black women.[10]

Cone offers suggestions regarding the silence of black theologians in reference to the exclusion of black women in the black theological enterprise. According to Cone there are some black male theologians "who are blatantly sexist" and thereby reflect the dominant culture in this regard.

> Others regard the problem of racism as the basic injustice and say that feminism is a middle-class White woman's issue. Still others make the controversial claim that the Black woman is already liberated.... Among professional theologians and

10. James H. Cone, "Introduction" in Gayraud S. Wilmore and James H. Cone, *Black Theology: A Documentary History, 1966–1979,* 363.

preachers as well as seminary and university students, few Black men seem to care about the pain our Black sisters claim that we inflict on them with our sexist behavior. If we expect to be taken seriously about our claim to love them, must not our love express itself in our capacity to hear their cry of pain and to experience with them their mental and physical suffering?[11]

In the attempt to connect with black women who have been rendered invisible by black theologians Cone sounds condescending as he suggests that black theologians should show black women some love by listening to their cries and be willing to embrace their pain. Cone is not yet willing to deal with sexism in black theology: the fact that black women are excluded as thinkers, as theologians in their own right. Cone misses an opportunity to point to the structural relationship between racism and sexism. His preoccupation with racism seems to provide blinders that prevent him from taking with full seriousness the interconnectedness of racism, sexism, and classism. Another way of identifying this difficult place in which Cone stands is to acknowledge his failure to sufficiently point to the relationship between the particular and the universal in theological discourse and in classroom practice. "As is always the case, it is difficult for people to recognize the significance of a particular form of experience when it does not arise from their own lives. My attempt to recognize the importance of women's experience in theology is found in the classes I teach at Union.... My earlier books ignored the issue of sexism; I believe now that such an exclusion was and is a gross distortion of the theological meaning of the Christian faith."[12] While Cone is correct in not wanting to subsume the particular in the universal and thereby lose the specificity of his analysis of racism, the challenge is how to allow the particular to provide a window through which others are able to see that their oppression and need for liberation is taken seriously. To respond to the exclusion of black women from black theological discourse with the assertion that black men must love them and listen to their cries is not yet to take them with sufficient seriousness.

---

11. Ibid., 363, 365.
12. Cone, "The Gospel and the Liberation of the Poor," 165.

This seems to be the assessment of womanist theologian Jacquelyn Grant in her important article "Black Theology and the Black Woman." Grant begins by pointing out the importance of a theological analysis that honors the interrelationship of racism, sexism, and classism. To highlight any one of these perspectives is to refuse to press for authentic liberation. Grant enquires:

> Where are Black women in Black theology? They are in fact, invisible. . . . In examining Black Theology it is necessary to make one of two assumptions: (1) either Black women have no place in the enterprise, or (2) Black men are capable of speaking for us. Both of these assumptions are false and need to be discarded. They arise out of a male-dominated culture which restricts women to certain areas of the society. In such a culture men are given the warrant to speak for women.[13]

Grant exposes black theology and the main reasons for the invisibility of black women in black theology. According to theologian Grant one word gets to the heart of the matter: patriarchy — the subordination of women to a male worldview, the attempt of men to act and speak for women. Patriarchy manifests itself in the notion that men are superior to women because women are given to emotionality and intuition while men are given to reason and intellect. "Just as White women formerly had no place in White theology — except as the receptors of White men's theological interpretations — black women have had no place in the development of black theology. By self-appointment, or by the sinecure of a male-dominated society, black men have deemed it proper to speak for the entire black community, male and female."[14]

Professor Grant is very helpful in describing a great deal of the practice that informs teacher-student relationships in the classroom. Black theology in particular as it relates to the black woman and white theology in general as it engages pedagogy are guilty of ways of relating and instruction in the classroom that do not honor the contributions of its participants. According to Grant, black and white

---

13. Jacquelyn Grant, "Black Theology and the Black Woman" in Wilmore and Cone, *Black Theology: A Documentary History 1966–1979*, 420.
14. Ibid.

theologians deny women the opportunity and fail to affirm their ability to think theologically. This is a problem in many classrooms in departments of religion and in theological seminaries that instructors whether white or black men tend to arrogate to themselves this ability to speak for women and thereby speak for God. Grant on the one hand faults black theologians for the sin of imitation. "Black men must ask themselves a difficult question. How can a white society characterized by Black enslavement, colonialism, and imperialism provide the normative conception of women for Black society?"[15]

Grant proposes another problem that informs pedagogy. If theology proffered by white theologians that undergirds the patriarchal structure of society is taken over by black men, why should black women think that this could be for their liberation? "If Black men have accepted those structures, is there any reason to believe that the theology written by black men would be any more liberating of black women than white theology was for white women?"[16] The way forward is to put "new wine in new wineskins." Grant reminds us that although black theology purports to be a theology of the black religious experience the problem has been that black women's experience was excluded. It is precisely at this point Grant indicates that something new is needed.

## Pedagogy as an Invitation to Love God

In her classic text *White Women's Christ and Black Women's Jesus,* Grant points out that the oppression of women in church and society led women to ask as their central question, "What has Jesus Christ to do with the status of women in church and society?" This question is a paraphrase of the question Jesus asked his disciples, "Who do you say that I am?" Grant indicates that for a long time men have sought to answer this question for women, but this must not continue, as women have to answer this from their own experience. In the past, women have allowed men to say who Jesus is for them, thereby denying the validity of their own experience. The problem is

---

15. Ibid., 421.
16. Ibid., 421, 422.

not merely that men have suggested answers to this question but they have sought to give definitive answers.

> Since man is limited by his social context and interests, Jesus Christ has been defined within the narrow parameters of male consciousness. That is to say, the social context of the men who have been theologizing has been the normative criterion upon which theological interpretations have been based. What this has meant is that Jesus Christ consistently has been used to give legitimacy to the customary beliefs regarding the status of women.[17]

Grant calls attention to the importance of black women's experience as a pedagogical resource. The importance of women's experience as source and resource for education cannot be overestimated as it places women in a position to teach and to initiate an exodus from traditions that thwart their human flourishing. It is precisely at this point that Grant's emphasis on women's experience as a basis for talk about God and pedagogy proffers an ethic of care as the next step.

The focus on care for self and neighbor highlights pedagogy as an invitation to love God. We noted earlier in Leviticus 19 that pedagogy as love for God included the commandment to love the stranger. And in Mark 12:30–31, as Jesus paraphrases Deuteronomy 6:4–5, he points out that love for God includes love for self and neighbor. It seems to me then that with black theology's emphasis on love for strangers as it tackles the stubborn reality of racism, and with womanist theology's focus on the need to isolate and identify women's experience as a source for talk about God and pedagogy as it takes on patriarchy, we are led in a new way to engage pedagogy as an invitation to love God. Love for God includes the critic as stranger, self, and neighbor. Pedagogy informed by the love of God challenges us to examine who is excluded in the context of teaching and learning. Each participant is invited to bear witness from experience of what it means to practice the love of God.

---

17. Jacquelyn Grant, *White Women's Christ and Black Women's Jesus*, 63–64.

*Part Two*

# Contextualizing
# the Curriculum

# Chapter 6

# International and Cross-Cultural Courses

## CHANGING THE CONTEXT

### David O. Jenkins

"Why have you come here?" Martyr asked.

It was the first time I had paid much attention to this forty-year-old, soft-spoken campesino. Although we gathered at his home three times a day for meals, although he had been the spokesperson for the community and welcomed us the night we arrived in his remote Honduran village, my attention had been focused on my students, watching and wondering how they were experiencing such disorientation and discomfort.

We were a mix of seminary and undergraduate students, hosted by a Honduran ecumenical ministry called La Comisión Cristiana de Desarrollo (The Christian Commission for Development). The organization had brought us to this village of El Limón (literally, "the lemon"), a community of thirty families clinging to the side of a mountain nearly a mile above the serpentine green river below. The ten-day spring-break trip was the "experiential" component of a semester-long class called "The Theologies and Ecclesiologies of Honduras." We had read our share of liberation theology, including studies of base communities, villages such as El Limón that relied on lay leadership for weekly worship and reflections on Scripture rooted in their day-to-day realities.

The village had decided to build a community center, a multi-purpose cinder block building with a tin roof and a few square windows. They had great visions for its future use: a clinic, should a doctor or dentist ever visit this remote community; a gathering place for the campesinos/as (farmers) to discuss land use and new laws governing land ownership and production; a room large enough for all of the community's women to meet for training on health care, nutrition, child care, and women's rights.

Without electricity, machinery, or even a road accessing the village, the community center had to be built by hand with simple tools and local resources. The cinder blocks had been made down at the river using the sand from the riverbed, but the task now was to carry these rough, heavy blocks straight up the mountain to the construction site. The steep trail snaked through sugar cane and corn fields, through open grazing land, under the scorching sun. This region of Honduras is always hot and always humid.

Although most of the students were young and fit, none of us was accustomed to such strenuous climbs in such intense heat. Book bags filled with textbooks didn't compare to the weight of two cinder blocks cutting into our hands and shoulders. We simply couldn't go far without stopping for shade and water. Our own rivers of sweat drew flies.

It was during one of these frequent breaks that Martyr, our guide up the mountain, asked us this question, "Why have you come here?"

I puffed up like a proud parent waiting for my students to reply with all the wisdom of two months of reading and classroom conversation. We had studied Honduran religious, political, and cultural history, had read some of the most influential Latin American theologians, had worshipped with local Latino congregations near campus, had watched videos and read novels, plays, and poetry. We were not like other tourists, not like other mission teams or even other seminary travel seminars. We were prepared for this question.

Before any of us could embarrass ourselves with a reply, Martyr answered his own question. "You came here hoping to *observe* our poverty and our faith. You came hoping to build a *community center* for us. You didn't know that we are building the kingdom of God."

We were thankful to sit in this shade long enough to hear the history of El Limón, how the women and men risked their lives to claim this rocky spit of land, how a young priest then came to live with them for six months, reminding them of God's incarnation among the poor.

El Limón became a base community, making sense of the need for a community center. In his own kind manner, Martyr instructed us, deconstructed us, and helped us construct a more coherent theology of poverty, a more coherent Christology, and a more critical self-understanding of ourselves as U.S. Americans, Christians (*his* sisters and brothers), and future pastors or lay leaders. On some levels, Martyr knew us better than we knew ourselves. Fifteen years later every sweaty student under that shade tree remembers that conversation, remembers Martyr.

Memory, a building block of religious identity, community, and education itself, was shaped for us by thirst, fatigue, heat, and sweat, the sound of Martyr's voice and the sight of his gentle, sunburned face. His teaching lodged in our bodies in the same places where the cinder blocks cut into our flesh and the blisters rose in our boots. It also lodged in between and among us — that is, it lodged in our communal experience and communal memory.

Fifteen years later I returned to that village with a class of seminarians from Candler. The village still didn't have electricity, so it requested help purchasing and installing a solar-powered generator which could run a corn grinder. Grinding corn is women's work in Latin America. Long before the men and children wake up, the women rise in the dark to build fires, make coffee, and prepare corn tortillas. They grind corn three times a day, every day. A solar powered grinder could save the women hours of hard daily labor, injuries to their hands and wrists, and lost sleep. It could also power a light bulb for the sole schoolteacher who could then read after sunset, grade papers, prepare lesson plans.

When the solar panels had been installed on the roof of an empty adobe shed, when the gray metal and white plastic grinder had been hooked-up to the generator and we were ready at long last to turn it on for the first time, charged with excitement and anticipation, the women in the village stopped us. One of them filled a small bucket with water, then together they "baptized" the grinder, generator, solar panels. It was a sacred moment. I remembered Martyr's theological claims about the incarnation of Christ among the poor. I believe that none of the seminarians crammed into that small shed on a steamy hillside in rural Honduras will ever forget that ritual. Those women helped make sense of our baptism.

These women were theologians. They were "doing" theology. With Martyr and many other lay leaders in El Limón, they embodied theological claims. One seminarian made the insightful links between the embodied theology of these base communities and his own embodied theological formation in this new context. He wrote:

> One [of my journal entries] was a section on embodiment. I recorded what I saw, heard, smelled, tasted, and felt. My whole person was engaged, not just my intellect. Shouldn't theology be done with the whole person in mind? I was faced with the stark reality of these persons, their words, how they looked and felt to me, the smells and tastes of their world. I heard their words and singing, but I also heard hope in their stories, sadness in their singing, anger and melancholy, as well as senses of relief. The proximity to concrete reality reinforces the notion that theology must be done for the concrete. If I am to do theology, it must be done with attention to the practical — indeed it must be done *for* the practical. Personally this is how I perceive the vocation of the theologian. Being there makes theology concrete. We saw how the abstractions of love and justice demand concrete form — especially if they are to be Christian in any sense.

As illuminated in this student's journal entry, students' *physical, social, and emotional* experiences in these international and cross-cultural settings help unearth the layered and complex forms of theological education, learning, and knowing. Their experiences of these new contexts, their relationships with people in these communities, their membership in a community of learners (the class itself, composed of the students and teachers who have traveled together), and their communal remembering, converge in ways that lead to formation and transformation. Each of these new concrete realities — people, relationships, place, and experience — contributes to emerging questions: Who does theology? What is theology for? *Who* is theology for? What does it mean to be Christian? Who do others say that I am?

A good international or cross-cultural class experiences internal and external collaboration of learning, rather than individual competition, which is often the norm in the Western modes of education. The professor is not an expert in these new contexts. Instead, the community residents, even the children, are the teachers and collaborators in the shared learning with the seminary class. Theology, even meaning itself, resides in the place, people, relationships, practices, shared worship, work, and meals. It takes a village to discover meaning.

One seminary student observed and experienced this new way of communal learning when she traveled to Cuba as part of a seminary class. The twenty participants were an equal number of faculty and students. As with the course on Honduras, the class gathered regularly for months before and after the spring-break trip to discuss readings on Cuban political, social, and religious history, as well as current trends in Cuban theology. Jessica Smith, the seminary student, had already studied Paulo Freire in her religious education class, so the vocabulary and concepts of liberative education were familiar to her when she wrote the following:

> In terms of seminary education, most seminarians view their professors through the lens of being a student. We, the students, collect or "bank" information and knowledge from the expert professor. The professor sets the parameters of the encounter, and the student responds to that controlled environment. But something happens to that classroom relationship when the student and professor journey to a place together. Theology looks differently and behaves differently when the context becomes a new setting for everyone. When we actually embody a community where persons are understood as more than professors and students, we make a statement about what we believe. We believe that our knowledge and power are elements of our more primary identity as fellow human beings.

Each time I travel with students I voluntarily step into the (shared) role of learner with them. Even if I have more formal education, even if I've been there before, and even if I have longstanding relationships with people in this place, the context transforms the teacher-student relationship. The expertise of the two *communities* — the group of seminarians and the residents of the community that welcomed the class — is what is dynamic. In El Limón, for instance, after only a few days of being in the village, students stopped asking the professor to interpret their experiences or respond to questions and concerns. They turned instead to Martyr, to other residents of the community, and to one another.

One could overhear conversations in the kitchen where several students assisted the women of the village with preparing meals and boiling water. The students raised sophisticated theological questions with the women in the village arising from the context — questions of theophany, soteriology, justice. Beside a pot of black beans boiling on an open fire in a home with dirt floors and no potable water, serious theological conversations occurred that shaped both communities. This theological formation occurred in more obvious places, too, as both communities gathered each evening to sing, read and interpret Scripture, share testimonies, and reflect on the day's work.

It can be a vulnerable place for seminary professors to inhabit. Within these new contexts it takes sensitive navigation of the new relationships with students. Professors not only share the learner's role with students, but also latrines, backbreaking work, contaminated water, new food and language. Often the students' strengths, wisdom, stamina, relational skills, and capacity to receive hospitality far outshine those capacities and skills of the professor. This is often the case in contextual education whether the context is a rural community in Latin America, a homeless shelter not far from campus, or a congregation with practices and doctrines unfamiliar to students and professors alike.

Jessica Smith rightly noted the theological claim implicit in this communal contextual learning. Several years after returning from Cuba, Smith wrote:

> I don't think I realized it at the time, but our group of professors and students were making a radical statement about who God is and who we are by traveling together to Cuba. Theologically, by living and traveling together we were acting out of a sense that God abides in and among us all, and we seek relationship with God through seeking to know one another. These scholars

of theology, preaching, and ethics were placing themselves with and among students, willing to be a source of knowledge, but also be embodied companions in a traveling community. We did not leave our identities as scholars and students behind when we traveled together. But we created a more dynamic, fluid relationship as fellow human beings seeking to know one another and God.

This is one of the many ways international and cross-cultural courses can offer students new models of theological education, as well as new models of mission teams and congregational outreach, social justice, and urban ministries. Many pastors who lead such international or domestic mission teams do so with the kind of arrogance that disregards local leadership. These pastors bring capital, administrative skills, professional expertise, and other resources into poorer communities, but also harmful assumptions about the lack of social capital, local leadership, and resources inherent in these poorer communities. They make these assumptions based not only on bad experiences of previous mission teams, but also from a lifetime of education in which those patterns of leadership and teaching forge disrespect for learners and communities, especially poorer communities in which many local leaders and residents don't have "higher" education.

The significance of the local community as context for theological formation was not lost on any student. David Lower, another member of the seminary class that visited El Limón, commented about that experience:

Their survival has depended on their living in community with one another, sharing resources and responsibilities. I did not appreciate the gravity or the potential of community until I arrived in El Limón. Their leader Martyr spoke so passionately about the story of El Limón, about its struggles and the triumphs that the people had made together. While I always viewed "community" as a desirable togetherness, the people of El Limón clearly thought of community as a means by which grace and survival entered their lives. While a different context allowed me to witness the transformative power of hope in community, I also learned valuable lessons about the challenges of community building and sustaining. Sin and self-interest pose great threats to a community of self-giving, whether that community is in Honduras or downtown Atlanta.

Even when these trips last only a week or two, the intensity of these experiences affords opportunities not easily afforded by other contexts. It is because of the intense nature of these cross-cultural experiences that there is the possibility of developing a community among the students and faculty. There are many values associated with this experience, all of which will benefit the students as they move from seminary into positions of congregational and community leadership, but many of those values will be immediately beneficial to the students during their seminary years.

There is also the possibility of real relationships, even friendships, between the seminary students and the community hosting the class. Receiving hospitality from another community, sharing daily chores and hard work around a common goal, playing with children, sharing meals, worshipping together, exchanging stories of family and faith, from sunrise to sunset, lay the groundwork for friendships to develop. These are the ordinary elements of any new friendship. Even if these relationships are short-lived, the intensity of those friendships holds transformative possibilities familiar to all of us. We have all been changed by our friendships.

Debbie Camphouse, a former seminarian fluent in Spanish and familiar with Latino/a cultures, participated in a cross-cultural course called "The Church on the Border." Students and faculty traveled to the U.S.-Mexico border to listen to and stay in the homes of Mexicans who worked in factories on the Mexican side or worked with people trying to cross into the United States to find work or be reunited with family. In a brief encounter with Mariela, a fourteen-year-old mother from Oaxaca, Debbie was changed. "Being able to meet people and ask questions," she wrote, "was more significant and more profound than simply reading the same material in a book because it forces you to put a face with a name and a story. And that *relationship* becomes the true impetus for creating change in the world." Debbie made the connection between the relationships with those who are living another reality than hers and the transformation that occurred in her as a result of that human relationship. That young mother's story, face, emotion, and honest engagement, moved Debbie to action. Debbie's current leadership of a Hispanic congregation in California, her lobbying efforts around immigration reform, and her particular theological convictions about the work of the church in the world were shaped and inspired by a short-lived relationship with Mariela.

It is most common and comfortable for us to forge relationships with those most like ourselves, relationships that can reinforce our worldviews, habits, and convictions. What these cross-cultural experiences offer students is the opportunity to forge relationships with those who are living a very different experience of the world. It is these relationships — with those both like and unlike ourselves — that change and transformation is often possible. This is usually uncomfortable, but that is when and where the growth occurs. As Debbie observed about herself, "I have traveled in many places, seen poverty and wealth, and been exposed to a variety of people, and yet Honduras still pushed me to go deeper. I believe it is in the 'going deeper' and being uncomfortable that produces real and significant change in a person's life. We must step outside of our paradigm if we ever wish to change the one we're in."

The task of becoming friends with those quite unlike ourselves requires students to develop certain skills. These skills, critical for any ministry of reconciliation and faithful leadership, are often already embodied in those we meet in these other contexts. They are survival skills for marginalized people. Once again, they become our teachers.

It is also within these new contexts and relationships that new hermeneutical practices are discovered. The host community functions as sacred text while students apply their exegetical skills to places and people as well as biblical passages. As an example, our class traveled to the border in early January when the lectionary readings included the flight to Egypt. As students encountered men and women on the border fleeing their homes in search of work, safety, hope, and family, they asked new questions of the biblical text. Who in Egypt helped Joseph find a job? Who helped Mary find kosher food? What kind of parents would let their children play with baby Jesus, or what local school board would encourage this undocumented foreigner to attend school? Simultaneously, questions about the nature of the church were raised. Is the church always in Diaspora? As our denominations become institutionalized (and institutionalized within neatly defined national borders), what vital characteristics of church are lost? How can we retain the sense of being pilgrims in the world? How can we live as a global, universal church in ways that honor these relationships with sisters and brothers in El Limón? How do my baptismal vows initiate me into this global church in ways that challenge and qualify my allegiance to any nation-state? These sorts of questions usually emerge as a result of personal relationships, not theoretical discourse. I encounter Martyr as my brother in Christ. That encounter has profound implications for my identity and my political practices as a citizen of a church rooted in the United States.

The intensity of these relationships in these uncomfortable contexts calls for a practical integration of social analysis with theological formation. It happens quite naturally. Power, wealth, race, gender, abilities/disabilities are critical considerations for students on these trips as they are confronted with disparities seldom experienced in relationship. These realities are raised within the lived experiences of communities unlike their own. Injustice has a face, smell, sometimes a taste and sound as students tell stories from the communities they visited. During her seminary trip to Cuba Jessica Smith made observations about U.S. foreign policy she never acknowledged before, observations inspired when people there told their stories of malnutrition as a result of the U.S. embargo. Vance West, one of the seminarians who traveled to the border, claimed "confrontation with the concrete realities of their world demonstrated the bankruptcy of neat theologies that have little to do with life as it is lived. Certain unexamined ideas about God's providence and our responsibility to civil government simply will not do when confronted with the reality we saw in Arizona and Mexico."

Finally, the intensity of this immersion experience engages students as whole people in ways that lead to transformation, which, I would argue, is the primary goal of theological education. Three years after returning from El Limón, David Lower wrote:

> Immersion in another context was vital to my transformative
> education. I had to encounter people who embodied Christian

faith in the heart of struggle. I had to see struggle in people's faces and hands. I had to hear hope and ultimate victory declared and sung by life-cracked voices in order to grasp what the transformative power of Christ's gospel is all about. Only in another context, one which is entirely strange to me, am I able to witness the depth of human struggles and the height of human hopes, and experience the present, transformative power of Christ working to traverse the distance between them. This is charged gospel, the kind that jolts you, and to hear and feel this message in a poor farming village is to be transformed by it. I have had many "formative" experiences in my life, like reading a powerful book that helped me to think and speak more clearly. What education by immersion in a Central American village provided me, though, was one of the rare "transformative" experiences that I now view as a vital element in my theological education.

I have argued for the values of international and cross-cultural courses, formative and transformative contextual education experiences. As they create new kinds of learning communities and allow for the possibility of friendship between distinctive communities — that of the seminary class and the community hosting the class — transformation of both communities of people is inspired. These communities and courses shape the theological memory of students while it calls them to new self-understanding, new forms of community and congregational leadership, and renewed commitments to justice.

# Chapter 7

# A Formula for Contextual Theology

LOCAL + GLOBAL = CONTEXTUAL

*M. Thomas Thangaraj*

Before joining the faculty of Candler School of Theology in 1988, I had worked as a theological teacher in India for several years. When I began my theological teaching in 1971, there was in Asia, and especially in India, a clear call to "contextualize" both one's theology and the prevailing theological education. This call was introduced and promoted by Dr. Shoki Coe of Taiwan, who at that time was the director of the Theological Education Fund of the World Council of Churches. As theological teachers, we focused on constructing uniquely Indian Christian theology and a peculiarly Indian form of theological education. Robin Boyd, who had worked in India as a missionary scholar for many years, brought out a book titled *An Introduction to Indian Christian Theology* in 1969. This book made us fully aware of various attempts by Indian Christians to articulate a theology that is contextual to India and linked us to the rich heritage of contextualized theology in India. Thus my career as a theological teacher began with a commitment to "contextualization."

As a professor of World Christianity, I was given a mandate to widen the minds and perspective of students at Candler, introduce them to the life of the churches outside the United States and offer them a global consciousness that sets them free from their parochial understandings of the Christian theological enterprise. My appointment to the faculty of Candler was part of a larger program called globalization of theological education of the Association of Theological Schools in the United States and Canada. I was invited to

98

create courses that would assist students to grow in "global" consciousness. I began to teach courses such as "The Church's Mission in a Pluralistic World," "Trends in Ecumenical Theology," "Images of Christ in World Christianity," "Doing Theology in a Global Context," and "Theological Responses to Religious Pluralism." In a way, my career as a theological teacher moved from "contextualization" to "globalization." It seemed like a shift in my pedagogical direction and method.

Was it, in fact, a shift, as far as my teaching was concerned? It was not. In India, I was inviting my students not to be satisfied with or shaped by theologies that were developed in the West; rather, they should seek out a contextual theology that grows out of and is constructed in the midst of contextual concerns and needs. This means it is not enough to read the writings of Karl Barth, Paul Tillich, the Neibuhrs, and other Western theologians. But they should soak themselves also in the theologies of Nehemiah Goreh, P. Chenchiah, Brahmabandhab Upadhyaya, A. J. Appasamy, and other Indian theologians. Here at Candler, I am doing the same thing — asking my students not to be content with knowing Western theology but to delve into the theological riches in other parts of the world, especially India.

Was my teaching, then, different from my colleagues who were focused on contextualization? It looked different in the beginning because of this: I seemed to be inviting students into a global context and thus drawing them away from their own local contexts, while my U.S. American colleagues were asking them to intensely focus their attention on local contexts. However, the situation has changed now. A process of globalization has taken place. Robert Schreiter, a Roman Catholic theologian in Chicago, describes this new situation as a combination of two processes, namely, extension and compression.[1] First, globalization has extended the benefits of modernity to every part of the globe. Second, globalization has compressed the world into a small village. Peoples, cultures, and languages have been brought in close proximity to one another in a compressed manner. In a way, local and global have been compressed into one reality. This

---

1. Robert Schreiter, *A New Catholicity: Theology between the Global and the Local.*

means, then, that we can no longer separate the local and the global; rather, we need to see our local in global terms and the global in local terms. Our local is not simply local anymore, and therefore our being faithful to our local context involves global elements. Similarly the global is not simply global; it has its own local manifestations. Thus, the context has taken a new shape. Let me express this new context in a formula: Local + Global = Contextual. What follows is an illustration of how this formula functions within a course titled "Images of Christ in World Christianity," which I have been teaching at Candler for many years.

In preparation for that exercise, let me give you an outline of the course. This course is planned to be a symphony in five movements.[2] The first movement is called "Acknowledging Tradition," in which students are introduced to the multiple ways of imaging Christ and the salvation offered in Christ in the cumulative tradition of the Christian church. They also come to know how certain images have come to dominate the scene. The second is "Resisting Domination," which deals with the African American, feminist/womanist, and non-Western resistance to the dominant "blue-eyed, blond-haired Jesus." Next comes a section titled "Affirming Plurality," which aims to show how in resisting domination one should protect oneself from idolatrous tendencies by affirming a plurality of images of Christ. The fourth section is titled "Nurturing Imagination" and examines hymns, poems, paintings, sculptures, and movies as expressions that nurture the imagination of one who images Christ. The final part of the course addresses the tensions that this whole exercise creates in the minds of the students and for their pastoral ministry. It is titled "Encountering Tensions." Two options are given to the students with regard to the final examination. They are:

*Option 1:* You may choose to write a paper on your own image of Christ. This paper should include a description of the image that you propose (this need not be totally original; it can be one of the existing images of Christ that is meaningful to you), and a defense of that image of Christ as helpful, appropriate,

2. This particular arrangement emerged when Ted Brelsford, as a doctoral student and my teaching assistant for this course, engaged me in reorganizing the course.

or adequate on the basis of biblical, theological, and contextual arguments. And you may use a set of criteria as well to defend your image of Christ as a helpful image. The contextual arguments may be offered with a description of the context in which the relevance of this image is discussed.

*Option 2:* You may choose to create an "art" piece, such as painting, poem, play, music, sculpture, collage, and so on. The piece should be accompanied by a commentary that explains why you did what you did, what this image means, and how you will defend this particular image as a helpful and appropriate image on the basis of biblical, theological, and contextual arguments similar to Option 1.

The course opens with *Head of Christ* — a painting of Christ by Warner Sallman in the 1940s, which gained popularity all over the world in a short period of time. Millions of copies of this painting are reproduced every year and sold in every part of the world. When I show this picture and mention "Let me present to you the Jesus we know," I get at least two responses. One, students are all surprised by its universal popularity; they find it difficult to believe that Indian Christians love and adore this picture. The other response is that both Anglo-American and African American students distance themselves from Sallman's painting and almost disown it. "That is not how I see Jesus," most of them would say.

This exposure to Sallman's *Head of Christ* is followed by a flood of images of Christ from different parts of the world, including local African American and feminist/womanist images of Christ. Every class session begins with a barrage of images projected onto the screen. While such a variety of images of Christ are shown, I keep inviting the students to "revel" in the plurality of images. The students are specifically asked to lay aside normative questions, such as "Is this an appropriate image?" "Is this a biblically and theological acceptable one?" They are also encouraged not to ask, "Will it preach?"[3] The shock of plurality often prevents students from

---

3. With a large number of final year students enrolling in this course, the question of pastoral applicability tends to be foremost in their minds.

"reveling" in it, and the ban on judging the images compounds their anxiety over normative claims. Overall there is an enormous amount of intellectual and emotional disturbance. In the midst of such disturbance and confusion, three stages of learning take place. These stages do not necessarily take place in a serial order as I have placed them in this essay; even in a single class session, a student may experience all the three stages in one particular order or another.

## The Stage of Dislocation

The bombardment of a variety of images of Christ and the confusion that ensues make students wonder where they are in relation to each of these images. There is a dislocation of context. When Sallman's head of Christ was projected on to the screen, most of the students knew their location or their context in relation to that picture. But when a barrage of images was introduced, they found themselves transported to a variety of contexts. One day they find themselves in the midst of African Americans in their attempts to image Christ as black, the next day they are with the feminists who ask for a Sophia Christ, and the following day they stand alongside the African American women who are imaging Christ as a poor black woman. Every time this happens, they are transported to a different context and an acute form of dislocation happens, both intellectually and emotionally.

When Third World images are presented with accompanying descriptions of Third World contexts, the students find themselves dislocated culturally. The images of Christ offered in Robert Schreiter's *Faces of Jesus in Africa* appear strange to most of the American students. They can understand and appreciate those images and "revel" in them only when they imaginatively transport themselves into the African context. Such transporting does lead to an experience of dislocation.

## The Stage of Disillusionment

The experience of dislocation is not a pleasant one; it is fraught with doubts, fears, and identity crises. What is an appropriate image? Do

I have the right image? Is it possible to come up with the most correct image of Christ? Who is to judge between the variety of images? If it is me, how may I judge? Are there criteria out there? These questions lead to an experience of disillusionment. This disillusionment is expressed in two ways. First, some students would plead for an "imageless" Christ. "Why do we need these visual images?" "Why not simply live with an imageless Christ of our heart and soul?" What is going on here is not intentional iconoclasm; rather it is an expression of one's frustration with a barrage of images and the complexity involved in judging between the different images. If having just a single and one-and-only image is problematic, then let me have none! Students who focus on the historicity of Jesus the Jew find it difficult to image Christ looking like a woman, or a Hindu guru, or a Chinese Buddhist monk. For such students a soft iconoclasm presents an easy way out of the mess that plurality creates.

Second, a sense of disillusionment is also exhibited when students push the question of the "essence" of what Christ stands for to the forefront. "Why worry about the non-essential features and squabble over them? Let's get to the essentials." This is the line of argument a lover of the essence of Christianity would take.

During these situations of disillusionment, what Mary Daly had to say about the ways in which men and women dismiss the feminist criticism of Christology is helpful. Students are introduced to the four forms of escape that she discusses, namely, universalization, particularization, spiritualization, and trivialization.[4] Universalization argues that if the fact that Jesus was not a woman is a problem, one should take note that he was not an Indian, or Chinese, or married man, or aged. Particularization dismisses the argument by maintaining that only some people have a problem with the traditional image and not all. Spiritualization demands that one focus on the "spiritual" character of Christ and the salvation he offers, and thus not worry about what Christ looks like. Trivialization would point out that one should rather be concerned about weightier matters and not worry about trivial ones such what Christ "looks" like!

---

4. See Mary Daly, *Beyond God the Father.*

## The Stage of Discernment

Dislocation and disillusionment finally lead to the stage of discernment. The student is able to discern his or her own context, appreciate the images of Christ in other contexts, and develop a set of criteria for evaluating the multiple images of Christ. The "reveling" in plurality that I mentioned earlier happens as the course comes to an end. It is, as Sugirtharajah has mentioned, a celebration of the gift of plurality. He writes, "The most challenging approach would be to accept these multiple images as a gift, scrutinizing their diversity and probing their meaning, purpose, and function, and above all, celebrating the gift."[5]

The process of discernment has two poles. The first is that of coming to grips with one's own context. What the exposure to the global does is to awaken the student to the local. When images from other parts of the world, which are intensely and intentionally "contextual" in character, are met by the students, that encounter kindles in them a keen awareness of their own context. One is enabled to discover and recognize the particularities and peculiarities of one's own contextual situation. Images from the global setting function as a sounding board for this discovery and recognition. Furthermore, an exposure to the global not only awakens the local but also challenges the local. The images from other contexts function as a prophetic critique of the local. This was clearly experienced when students discussed the role of the black Christ in white Christian communities. The black Christ functions as a critique of the dominant images of Christ among the whites. Similarly, the images from India may function as a critique of the black Christ.

Second, discernment involves discovering what the local can offer to the global as well. Coming to grips with one's own context enables the student to refrain from universalizing the local. Most often the dominant images of Christ in the global situation are products of a false universalism. When Sallman's *Head of Christ* is promoted as *the* image of Christ in contexts other than the West, sensitivity to the local is able to recognize and condemn the false universalism present in such a promotion. Moreover, sensitivity to the local prevents the

---

5. R. S Sugirtharajah, *Asian Faces of Jesus*, 259.

student from claiming any "global" cash value for his or her own image of Christ too.

One of the joys of teaching this course has been to witness the above mentioned two aspects of discernment in the final projects of the students. Let me mention a few. The real names of the students are replaced with fictional ones to protect their privacy.

## A Black Christ

Samson is an African American student who was clearly committed to a black Christ even before he enrolled in this course. Therefore, during class discussions he would ably argue for a black Christ. In a way, he was keenly aware of the needs and demands of his own African American context. The final project he chose was to carve a wooden relief of the face of Christ. He selected dark-colored wood and carved the face. It looked fully black and was indeed a black Christ. But his exposure to the global in the course would not allow him to sit comfortably with the image he had created. Samson felt compelled to find ways by which his image could be open to and inclusive of people other than African Americans. He spent hours and days contemplating this possibility and finally struck upon a wonderful idea. He ditched out chunks of wood from the cheeks of the face and in their places fixed pieces of mirror. Thus when people stood in front of his image, they not only saw a black Christ, they also saw their own face in it! An exposure to the global made him view his community as larger than the one that he came from, and sensitivity to the local enabled him to keep the African American focus of his image intact. His was truly a contextual image. Samson proved the formula: local + global = contextual.

## A Christ Chair

Nancy was enrolled in this course soon after the tragic death of her young and energetic daughter. What was foremost in her mind was her own context of pain and grief. She was looking for comfort and healing. Her local context was her own personal and biographical situation of loss and grief. As she watched images of Christ, one after another projected on to the screen in class sessions, she was beginning to see clearly her own peculiar and tragic context. Nancy began to experience a process of healing as well. Pain and relief, sorrow and comfort, illness and healing, and death and life became the global realities for her. For her final project, she decided to make a chair — a Christ chair — since she was herself a good carpenter. The chair had two arms shaped in the form of embracing hands. The back of the chair could be folded to the front in such a way that it could appear like a ladder to climb on. So for Nancy this was a chair that symbolized the loving embrace of Christ and Christ's bending forward to become the ladder for us to climb out of our sorrows and grief. In a powerful way Nancy demonstrated how her own context was a combination of the local and the global. She truly illustrated the formula: local + global = contextual.

## A Window into God

David was fascinated with the idea of Christ as a window into God. So for his project he chose to make three windows (each more than five feet tall) with glass. The glass in one window had transparencies with biblical texts pasted onto it; the other had images of Christ, again in transparencies; and the third one had pictures of peoples, events, landscapes, and others representing the world. The three windows could be placed facing one another in different ways. One arrangement would be to have the images of Christ at one end, the world at the other end, with the biblical texts in the middle. This would represent a view or imaging of Christ that starts with the world, examines the biblical witness, and constructs an image. Depending on the sequencing of the windows there is a variety in viewing Christ. Here is a student who is discerning the way in which the global and the local interact in constructing a contextual image of Christ. David has shown that the formula — local + global = contextual — holds true.

To conclude, let us revisit the idea of the new situation in which we find ourselves today. The population of the world today is 6.6 billion people, and such a vast population is now experienced as one single village. The words "global" and "local" have taken on different meanings now. They do not mean the same as they did a century ago. Local generally meant "here," and global "far away"; local meant "mono-everything" and global "multi-everything." Local meant "uniformity" and global "diversity." Local meant *swadeshi,*[6] and global "international." But today these words do not mean what I have listed above. The local has extended to the global and the global has invaded the local. In this setting, context cannot simply be local or global. It has to be both, in interaction with each other. This means, then, that there is not a big difference between the Americans and the non-U.S. Americans on the faculty. We are all involved in both the local and the global. It is not possible to teach biblical interpretation without taking into account the hermeneutical attempts by Christians in the so-called Third World. It is no longer desirable to teach the history of Christianity, limiting it to the history of the church in the West. The worldwide character of Christian faith should not be taught anymore without acknowledging and appreciating the worldwide character of other religions, such as Hinduism, Islam, Buddhism, and Judaism. Therefore, contextual theology and contextual theological education cannot but abide by the formula: local + global = contextual.

---

6. *Swadeshi* means "of one's own country," a phrase used by Mahatma Gandhi during the independence struggle in India.

# Chapter 8

# Christian Practices and Feminist Theological Formation

## DOING SAVING WORK

*Joy Ann McDougall and Claire Bischoff*

In her pioneering work on feminism and theological education, Rebecca Chopp coined the term "saving work" to describe a set of feminist practices that have been quietly transforming theological education and the church's life together.[1] Saving work signifies first of all the practice of "narrativity": a complex process by which women (and men) compose their lives anew through theological education, so to free themselves from prescriptive gender roles and to gain agency for identity formation. Saving work includes as well various practices of "ekklesiality" — Chopp's term for acts of lamentation and community formation, critical analyses of oppression and of symbol systems, and spiritual practices involving embodiment and connectedness. These ecclesial practices seek to denounce the sins of patriarchy while proclaiming the grace of new possibilities for just relationships with God, self, others, and the world.[2] Finally, saving work demands feminist theological reflection itself: the ongoing envisioning of Christian symbols and practices as a way of participating in God's saving activity for the world. Taken together, these practices constitute something more than an agenda for curriculum reform in theological schools — although they surely entail that as well. Feminist practices boldly reinterpret Christianity so as to renew the life of the church and its public witness to the world.

---

1. Rebecca S. Chopp, *Saving Work: Feminist Practices of Theological Education.*
2. See ibid., 77.

108

Surely there is no more urgent task to engage in saving work about than the doctrine of God.[3] This is due prima facie to the primacy of God as the "object" of theology. If Christian theology is about nothing else, it is surely about offering good news about God and God's relationship to the world. Doing saving work about the doctrine of God becomes all the more critical, however, once one realizes how this doctrine underwrites and ties together the other key aspects of the Christian faith, for example, theological anthropology, Christology, and ecclesiology. So, too, the doctrine of God provides the ultimate norms of love and justice that shape individuals' daily patterns of living and the church's common life of faith. As Elizabeth Johnson observes about the doctrine of the Trinity: it "functions"; "it powerfully molds the corporate identity of the Christian community, highlights its values, and directs its praxis."[4]

Recognizing the doctrine of God's wide-ranging implications, feminist theologians have challenged the sexist dimensions of Christianity's traditional "social-symbolic order," in which God is depicted as a supreme and transcendent male sovereign (for example, as the king, lord, or judge), while human society and nature are pictured in inferior female terms.[5] Once genders are positioned asymmetrically in this manner, feminists contend, Christianity lends sacred legitimacy to a patriarchal social order: men are free to represent God, Christ, and true humanity, while women symbolize fallen humanity and the church as passive recipients of divine grace. This divine-human economy diminishes women's personal agency, threatens their sense of self-worth, and subjugates them to the dominating will of others — divine or human.[6]

In light of the damaging history of effects of Christianity's social-symbolic order for women, feminist theologians have set to work

---

3. By "doctrine of God," I mean most generally those "communally inherited teachings" about the nature and agency of God that regulate the life of the Christian community. For this notion of doctrine and its extension in contemporary feminist theology, see Serene Jones, *Feminist Theory and Christian Theology: Cartographies of Grace*, 16–17.

4. Elizabeth A. Johnson, "To Let the Symbol Sing Again," 300.

5. Here I am trading on Chopp's notion of a "social-symbolic order" as a "patterning of certain values and principles" that structures "subjectivity, language and politics" in a given historical situation. For a fuller description of this idea, see Rebecca S. Chopp, *The Power to Speak: Feminism, Language, and God*, 14–15.

6. For a recent version of this feminist critique, see Daphne Hampson, *After Christianity*, esp. 119–68.

reforming the Christian doctrine of God. They ask how women's narratives, ecclesial practices, and theological traditions can remedy the androcentrism of the Christian doctrine of God, for example, its predominant male imagery for God or its models of divine love or power. How might the concrete realities of women, their joys and sufferings, contribute to new life-giving ways of speaking or reflecting about the nature of God? At the same time feminists look to a reformulated doctrine of God as the foundation for an alternative liberating vision of gender relations for men and women today. Can Christian speech about God become what Chopp calls "a discourse of emancipatory transformation," a proclamation of the Word that contributes to more just ways of living together?[7]

## *Teaching the Doctrine of God:*
## *Women's Voices Past and Present*

With the aim of participating in feminist saving work with the doctrine of God, we — a systematic theologian and religious educator — designed and taught a master's level seminar entitled "The Doctrine of God: Women's Voices Past and Present" at Candler School of Theology in the spring of 2006. Besides giving our students a solid grounding in the Christian doctrine of God, two feminist aims guided our methodology in the course. First, we wished to engage our students in reading women's past theological traditions in tandem with recent contemporary feminist and womanist discourse. Without claiming that women's theological voices are essentially or universally different from men's, we saw an urgent need for today's seminarians to gain firsthand knowledge of women's traditions. Be it Hildegard of Bingen's mystical visions of the Trinity or Zora Neale Hurston's fictional accounts of African American women's efforts to find a liberating God amid life-struggles, past women's theological traditions demonstrate that women have always been engaged in significant theological work — whether it has been institutionally recognized or not.[8]

---

7. Chopp, *The Power to Speak*, 7. For a superb survey of the different trajectories in feminist and womanist discourse about God, see Mary Grey, *Introducing Feminist Images of God*.

8. For an excellent introduction to women's theological traditions focused on the issue of gender and redemption in Christ, see Rosemary Radford Ruether, *Women and Redemption: A*

We view such a hermeneutic of retrieval as essential to feminist saving work. As systematic theologian Kathryn Tanner reminds her fellow feminists, theological traditions should be a "site of political contest" for feminists, not least because appeals to a valued past in Christian theology serve to authorize present and future practice: "Whoever controls the interpretation and designation of the past that authorizes present practice, gains the power to delimit what is authentically Christian, what is appropriate for a Christian to say and do."[9] In this light retrieving women's theological traditions is not about wresting a feminist blessing from the past, but about gaining the resources and the authority to craft the church's present and future tradition. By shifting women's theologies from the margins to the center of the church's received traditions, we sought to disrupt the patriarchal construction and transmission of Christian tradition, replacing it with a more gender-inclusive tradition to be passed on to coming generations.[10]

One other pedagogical aim drove the design of our seminar: to integrate a variety of Christian practices into the teaching of the doctrine of God. Here, too, theological and feminist commitments informed our turn to practices in the classroom. For one, along with many others in contemporary theological education, we sought to bridge the artificial gap that exists between the teaching of doctrine and students' formation in Christian practices in seminary education.[11] We envisioned a dynamic relationship between doctrines and Christian practices, and sought to cultivate in our students a lively awareness of their interdependence. Integrating Christian practices into teaching doctrine seemed particularly apropos of the women's historical traditions we were exploring. Most of these women had

---

*Theological History.* For an anthology of women's theological writings, see Amy Oden, ed., *In Her Words: Women's Writings in the History of Christian Thought.*

9. Kathryn Tanner, "Social Theory Concerning the New Social Movements and the Practice of Feminist Theology," in *Horizons in Feminist Theology: Identity, Tradition and Norms,* ed. Rebecca Chopp and Seila Greeve Davaney, 179–97, here 193.

10. For a more critical take of the notion of moving marginal traditions to the center, see Rebecca Chopp, "When the Center Cannot Contain the Margins," in *The Education of the Practical Theologian,* ed. Don Browning, David Polk, and Ian Evison, 63–76.

11. On the turn to praxis in theological education, see Chopp's detailed discussion in her *Saving Work,* 15–18. For the recent discussion on the interplay of doctrine and Christian practices, see the various essays collected in Miroslav Volf and Dorothy C. Bass, eds., *Practicing Theology: Beliefs and Practices in Christian Life.*

engaged in daily ritual practices of Bible study, prayer, and worship, or else some form of aesthetic religious expression. By introducing students to these women's ancient (and at times alien) religious practices, we hoped that they might appreciate more fully these women's lived theological wisdom.

As feminists, we were also committed to a praxis-oriented model of theological education, that is, one in which Christian practices not only form believers in the life of faith but also aim to transform their lives and their witness to the world.[12] Following Chopp among others, we understood the "habitus" of theological education as therefore involving diverse forms of knowledge — "not only of classical wisdom and of modern critical methods, but also emotional, aesthetic, affectional and spatial and empathetic learning."[13] By engaging students in Christian practices that involved their bodies, aesthetic sensibilities, and deepest passions, we sought to realize such a holistic model of theological education in our classroom.

One other rationale guided our integration of Christian practices into teaching the doctrine of God: we wished to engage the different cultural and denominational traditions of our students. The fourteen women and two men in our seminar represented a broad range of cultural backgrounds — that of the United States, South Korea, Brazil, Nigeria, and Ghana. Half of them belonged to various branches of the Methodist family, while the other half represented the Baptist, Presbyterian, Episcopal, and Roman Catholic traditions. By asking the students to lead the class in diverse Christian practices in tandem with the weekly readings, we provided a venue in which they could interpret these women's traditions in their own cultural idioms. We invited them explicitly into the process of inculturating women's theological traditions, so that they might more readily pass them on in their future ministries.

Our turn to practices in teaching Christian doctrine reflects our embrace of a contextual approach to theological education. Through the practices component of our pedagogy, we sought to thematize the various experiential horizons and cultural situations from which

---

12. Chopp, *Saving Work*, 17.
13. Ibid.

our students were engaging diverse women's theological traditions and each other's beliefs about God. Rather than treating our students' cultural differences as limitations to be transcended in the learning process, we looked to affirm them as the "location for the construction of meaning."[14] That is to say, we sought to identify what productive differences their personal narratives, ecclesial traditions, and cultural situations make to the style and substance of their theological reflection, and to our common endeavor of exploring new ways of thinking and naming God. By according to practices a certain priority in our pedagogy, we were also affirming a key principle of contextual education, namely, integrating the pursuit of theoretical knowledge and practical wisdom with the making of normative judgments. Rather than encouraging a priori judgments about the right ways of speaking about the Christian God, we invited students instead to participate in concrete practices in which they would try on and try out different ways of envisioning God with the expectation that such experience-based learning would help them identify their own normative beliefs about God.

## Situating Feminist Theological Formation: Teaching Christian Practices

Before looking close-up at a couple of our efforts to integrate Christian practices into the classroom, let us provide first an overview of the course syllabus and our different teaching strategies. The seminar opened with a session devoted to naming the theological, ethical, and existential issues raised by gendered language for God. Through reading short selections from Roberta Bondi, Mary Grey, and Elizabeth Johnson, students were acquainted with basic feminist questions about gender and Christian God-talk and had the occasion to discuss how gendered images for God intersected with their own lives and that of their church communities.

After this introductory session, we began a five-week unit devoted to retrieving past women's theological traditions. We looked first at

---

14. Ibid., 37.

the Scriptures, uncovering female imagery for God in the Old Testament and then debating the centrality of God the Father language to the New Testament witness. Taking a leap forward in time, we turned next to explore the writings of two women mystics, Hildegard of Bingen's *Scivias* and Mechtild of Madgeburg's *The Flowing Light of the Godhead*. We chose these two authors not only because they exemplify recently rediscovered medieval women's traditions, but also because the unusual genres of their respective work — mystical visions and erotic poetry — challenge students' notions about the normative style of academic theology. Moreover, Hildegard's and Mechtild's theologies diverge dramatically from one another, particularly in their understandings of divine love and the soul's relationship to the Trinity. By reading these authors back to back, we wished to dispel any prejudices that students might harbor about the nature of women's theological work, for example, it being more affective or less doctrinally rigorous than that of their male counterparts.

The second half of the course exposed students to different feminist and womanist voices on the doctrine of God. As our entrée into the current debate, we read first classic essays by Mary Daly on moving beyond God the Father, and by Carol Christ on why women need Goddess language. As a counterpoint, we then read Zora Neal Hurston's novel *Their Eyes Were Watching God* together with womanist theologian Katie Cannon's interpretation of her work. Hurston's novel provided the occasion not only to discuss fiction as a significant genre of African American women's theological writing but also to thematize how the theodicy question challenges Christian claims about the goodness and justice of God.

In the final five weeks of the course we took up different feminist proposals for construing God's nature and relationship to creation. We looked first at Sallie McFague's *Body of God: An Ecological Theology,* and explored how attitudes towards women, nature, and the social order are bound up with different gendered images and models of God. We then engaged three rival proposals for reconstructing classical trinitarian theology — those of Elizabeth Johnson, Janet Martin Soskice, and Sarah Coakley. By exploring these proposals in concert with one another, students quickly learned that there was no single feminist trinitarian orthodoxy, but rather a lively debate among feminists about how gender, the Trinity, and women's spiritual praxis relate to one another.

Our weekly class sessions were structured in the following way. The first two hours were run as a seminar, during which time the teaching team relied on traditional academic teaching strategies, i.e., assigned reading, writing, and common discussion. Each week one or two students prepared brief seminar papers focused on the readings and then served as resident experts along with the two instructors in leading our seminar discussions. The other students wrote a brief theological reflection on a central aspect of the week's reading, which provided them with a jumping-off point for participating in our common discussion.

For the final hour of the class, the seminar leaders were given the additional task of preparing and leading the seminar in a Christian practice. In describing this assignment to the students, the teaching team employed a broad definition of Christian practices.[15] Rather than prescribing a set of traditional Christian practices, we were committed to giving the students the latitude to experiment with different religious practices — be they ancient or modern, silent or spoken, kinetic or cognitive. This was in keeping with our twofold agenda of retrieving women's past theological traditions as well as inviting students to reimagine current ecclesial practices. The only stipulations we placed on the practice was that it be tied directly to the week's readings and that it could be accomplished during the final hour of our class.

One practice that exemplifies well our desire to revitalize women's past spiritual traditions was that of *lectio divina* or sacred reading, a practice that one of the instructors led during the week that we read Mechtild of Madgeburg's *The Flowing Light of the Godhead*. *Lectio divina* is a spiritual practice of praying the Scriptures and conversing with God traceable to the early patristic period. It is not theological

---

15. Following Craig Dykstra and Dorothy Bass, we defined Christian practices quite generally as "things Christian people do together over time to address fundamental human needs in response to and in the light of God's active presence for the life of the world." For this definition and their more recent christological revision of it, see their essay, "A Theological Understanding of Christian Practices," in Volf and Bass, *Practicing Theology*, 13–32, here 18.

study or exegesis but "reverential listening" centered in the heart.[16]
It begins with reading a selected biblical text slowly and attentively
multiple times and meditating on this particular word of God so that
it touches you deeply. After reading and meditating comes prayer,
which is understood both as a dialogue with God and as consecration,
as we allow the word of God to change us. *Lectio divina* concludes
with contemplation, where we silently rest in God's embrace. While it
traditionally has been practiced as a private and individual dialogue
with God, group forms of *lectio divina* have recently become more
widely practiced.

We seized hold of *lectio divina* for that week, because we saw significant resonances between this practice and Mechtild's spirituality.
For one, Mechtild's work, grounded as it is in her mystical visions
and special awareness of God's presence in her life, arises from the
same sort of consciousness of God's nearness that *lectio divina* invites. Furthermore, the contemplative goal of *lectio divina*, resting in
God's love, parallels what Mechtild describes in her writing as getting
beyond oneself. Because of these resonances, we decided to use selections from Mechtild's writings rather than a biblical text for our *lectio
divina*. By placing Mechtild's text in the context of common prayer,
we sought to help students to appreciate her writing for what it is —
a poetic rendering of one woman's encounter with God's presence —
and to engage with it based on this identification.

Our *lectio divina* was quite simple. We began in silence, concen-
trating on our breathing. As one student read a short passage from
Mechtild aloud twice, we attended to the words and phrases that
sprung to our attention and then reflected on them in the silence
that followed. To conclude this first round of reflection, we shared
aloud the word or phrase that had attracted us. We followed a similar procedure twice more. In the second iteration, we listened to the
text again, considered the question "Where does the content of the
reading touch my life today?" and shared one sentence in response.
Finally, in response to the third reading of the text we completed the
sentence "I believe that God wants me to...," speaking aloud any

---

16. Luke Dysinger, "Accepting the Embrace of God: The Ancient Art of Lectio Divina,"
available at *www.valyermo.com/ld-art.html*, May 16, 2007.

part of our reflection that we wished to share with the group. We concluded our *lectio* by praying aloud together a litany drawn from one of Mechtild's visions.

While we first selected *lectio divina* because of its resonances with Mechtild's spirituality, we also recognized it as a practice that could help bridge the distance to past women's theological traditions. Surmising that students may find it difficult to glean insight from unusual genres of theology, such as Mechtild's erotic poetry, we looked to *lectio divina* to assist the students both in bringing their imagination to the text and in reading the text in a new way. The practice of *lectio divina* begins the process of activating the imagination, by asking students to focus on words and images from the text that speak to their hearts and not to their heads. Attending to the text in silence frees the imagination to work so that students may hear and envision the text anew. As educator Maxine Greene explains, our imagination "allows us to break with the taken for granted, to set aside familiar distinctions and definitions."[17] Perhaps even more importantly, "imagination is what, above all, makes empathy possible,"[18] because imagination can be understood as "becoming a friend of someone else's mind, with the wonderful power to return to that person a sense of wholeness."[19] When the imagination is invoked, students may be better able to engage in and empathize with the unfamiliar and sometimes alien theological voices of the past, such as those of medieval women mystics.

Beyond inviting our students to approach Mechtild's writings imaginatively, we endeavored to demonstrate through *lectio divina* that there is more than one way to read theological texts. As Paul Griffiths argues in "Reading as a Spiritual Discipline," most graduate students have learned to read in an academic mode characterized by the technical skill of extracting meaning from written texts with increasing speed and acumen.[20] The teaching team assumed that the students probably had read Mechtild in this fashion to prepare for

---

17. Maxine Greene, *Releasing the Imagination: Essays on Education, the Arts, and Social Change*, 3.

18. Ibid.

19. Ibid., 38.

20. Paul J. Griffiths, "Reading as a Spiritual Discipline," in *The Scope of Our Art: The Vocation of the Theological Teacher*, ed. L. Gregory Jones and Stephanie Paulsell, 32–47.

class, and many were at a loss about how to interpret her theology. By engaging with Mechtild's writing in the *lectio divina,* the students practiced a more attentive and deliberate mode of reading, one that may be more appropriate than academic reading for understanding mystical theological texts. Further, as Griffiths observes, inasmuch as "reading may be a transformative spiritual discipline" students need to learn to read not just academically, but also in other modes that may better provide spiritual nourishment and challenge.[21] Knowing that one brief exposure to *lectio divina* would have a limited effect on the students, we also hoped that some might be encouraged through this practice to experiment with different ways of reading in their coursework, in their personal spiritual practice, and in their future ministries.

If *lectio divina* represents one of the traditional practices in which we engaged, making friendship bracelets exemplifies a contemporary cultural practice that two of the students adapted for the classroom setting. Inspired by that week's reading on friendship language in the Gospel of John, they arrived to class bearing skeins of colored embroidery thread. We were instructed to cut at least three equal-length threads of different colors, to knot the threads together, and to tape the knot to the table in front of us. Then the two leaders, with the help of a book about friendship bracelets, endeavored to teach us how to make the bracelets through a well-coordinated system of knots. As the leaders circulated, assisting us in learning the practice, we were instructed to discuss our own understanding of friendship with the person next to us.

The practice of making friendship bracelets was successful in many respects. By inviting us to engage our hands as well as our heads, the practice provided a pedagogical change of pace to the first two hours of class, which were spent largely in group discussion on texts. In the process, we also gained exposure to a popular practice widespread among adolescent women and one that resonates with the recent renaissance of women's stitch'n'bitch knitting groups. In creating space for informal conversation about friendship, this practice also helped foster friendly relations among class members, particularly since it

---

21. Ibid., 46.

gave students the opportunity to interact with someone new early in the semester.

There were obvious shortcomings to this practice as well. For one, the student leaders faced practical difficulties explicating this tricky, fine-detail process to a large group within the time-frame allotted. For the class members not familiar with making friendship bracelets, most of their time and attention were spent on learning the practice. This required one-on-one tutoring from the leaders and took away from the opportunity to engage meaningfully in conversation about friendship. The leaders also confronted a pedagogical difficulty that recurred with many of the student-led practices: they struggled to articulate the theological connection between the reading and the practice beyond drawing a very general correlation. In this case, it seemed as if we were making friendship bracelets simply because friendship was a major theme from the reading. This is not to say that making friendship bracelets was not an appropriate practice to engage in. The leaders, however, needed to reflect much more about how this particular practice embodied insights from the reading, and also how to encourage critical conversation about the dissonances between the understanding of friendship signified by these bracelets and that present in the Gospel of John.

The success of integrating practices into the feminist classroom became evident in our final class session, when five students collaborated to lead us in a well-crafted worship service that incorporated different aspects of Elizabeth Johnson's trinitarian theology, with which we concluded our class readings. That afternoon we gathered in the cramped choir room of the chapel to reflect on the Trinity in prayer and to celebrate our work together over the course of the term. We began by hearing a reading from Proverbs and invoking Spirit-Sophia using selections from Audre Lorde's poetry. We then prayed to Jesus-Sophia using the text of a Brian Wren hymn, listened to portions of the Gospel of John, offered prayers of the people in the form of artwork we had made throughout the class, and recited "Sophia's Prayer," taken from a New Zealand/Maori Anglican liturgy. We completed our trinitarian liturgical practice by praying to Mother-Sophia using Langston Hughes's "The Negro Mother," singing "Fairest Sophia," and hearing selected Scriptures focusing on the motherhood of God. We closed in benediction, praying aloud a love poem written by a Korean Buddhist and offering each other the sign of peace. Even though the service went longer than the scheduled class time, students and teachers alike lingered around to offer the peace and blessings to one another. The mood was joyful, as many felt and expressed the sense that we had just been part of a unique worship experience.

While bearing the recognizable elements of a traditional worship service, such as hymns from the UMC book of worship and selected Scripture readings, our final practice also integrated unorthodox women's theological resources. These elements reflected the students' different cultural and denominational backgrounds, their preferred genres of theological expression, and their varied gifts for ministry. Despite the wide variety of theological resources, our closing worship service devolved neither into cacophony nor into being just a theological smorgasbord. It maintained a center of theological gravity, inviting us all into a deeper reflection on the beauty, truth, and goodness of the trinitarian God with new imagery and lively ritual forms. In our eyes, the liturgy embodied just the kind of saving work that we had sought to achieve in teaching the course.

## *Pedagogical and Theological Gleanings: The Turn to Practices Revisited*

Incorporating Christian practices into teaching the doctrine of God provoked several unexpected pedagogical and theological challenges for us as the teaching team. These ranged from the most practical of issues, such as how to teach students to lead a group effectively in a religious practice, to the more complex questions of what constitutes excellence in Christian practices, and how one measures it in the classroom.[22] While space does not permit us to explore all of our pedagogical and theological gleanings here, we shall highlight a couple that have broader implications for teaching through practices in theological education.

---

22. For a recent discussion of "excellence in ministry and pastoral leadership," see Jackson W. Carroll and Becky R. McMillan, *God's Potters: Pastoral Leadership and the Shaping of Congregations*, 192–218.

First, the teaching team recognized that we needed to do more critical reflection on what we did (and did not) mean by Christian practices. Although we had invited students to experiment with alternative religious practices, we wondered in retrospect how our own understandings about what constitutes a core Christian practice influenced the assignment's design. Were there particular goals of spiritual formation or theological learning that we expected our weekly practices to achieve, and if so, had we articulated this implicit curriculum to our students? Finally, had we provided our students with adequate pedagogical support for these goals to be met?

In posing these questions, we discovered that we had proceeded inductively in designing the practices assignment. We asked our students to develop a religious practice that reflected the course materials, their cultural traditions, and their particular gifts for ministry, and were curious to see what imaginative practices would emerge. In many respects, our inductive approach to teaching Christian practices was the right pedagogical decision. The students clearly benefited from us not being overly prescriptive about what counted as a valid Christian practice or not. Over the course of the semester, a range of new ecclesial practices were experimented with, such as friendship bracelets as described above, storytelling groups, and a nature walk through our university neighborhood. Engaging in these unconventional practices helped not only build a powerful sense of community in the classroom, but also encouraged our students to be less wedded to traditional Christian practices in their ministry settings. To our surprise every single practice — even those that the teaching team considered not terribly successful — was named by at least one student in the course evaluations as a practice that she or he might use in her or his future ministry.

While we encouraged our students to try out nontraditional practices, we certainly had academic and theological expectations about this assignment. Most obviously, we required that our weekly practice be tied closely to the women's theological traditions that we were encountering. Just as a successful worship service has scriptural readings, hymns, prayers, and a sermon, all of which hang together thematically, so too we expected our religious practices to resonate richly with our written theological materials. As such, the sine qua non for a successful final hour of class was that the student leaders had done their reading and written assignments well — not to mention preparing the practice itself carefully. With this sort of preparation, the student leaders were better able to conceive of and lead a practice that was faithful to the week's reading and that deepened our theological engagement with it.

At a more profound level, we also expected that our weekly religious practices would contribute to our overarching feminist theological agenda, that is, of doing "saving work" with the doctrine of God. We hoped that these practices would in some small measure transform the personal narratives, the ecclesial practices, and the symbolic order with which Christians professed their beliefs about God. Given this ambitious theological agenda, we discovered that our weekly practices needed to do more than illustrate the week's reading or translate it into a different symbolic and cultural key. They needed to appeal to the students' imagination, challenge their theological convictions, and engage their deepest passions. Developing a successful practice required, therefore, not only considerable theological insight from our students, but also creativity and practical judgment.

Happily many of the students intuitively grasped our aims in integrating Christian practices into teaching the doctrine of God and required little help in practicing theology well. Their written work showed a deep understanding of the theological issues at stake in the readings, and they demonstrated creativity in developing a practice for our group — whether it took the form of a meditation, an artistic exercise, or a community-building activity. Others, however, clearly needed more guidance in developing a meaningful religious practice — surprisingly even when they were adapting a traditional Christian practice such as prayer or Bible study. Midway through the course, we realized that several of the students simply lacked the ministry experience and the teaching skills to lead a small group successfully in a religious practice. Next time around we vowed to give the students more pedagogical support in developing the practice for the classroom setting.

Another unexpected dimension of our feminist agenda with Christian practices emerged through teaching the course: the desire to nurture women's sense of pastoral authority. As theological educators, we are painfully aware that many women students struggle with "authoring" or "being authorized" in their calls to ordained ministry.[23] They struggle to claim publicly their calls to ministry or to receive official recognition for them from denominational officials. Moreover, women often enter seminary expressing ambivalence about being called out from their communities of faith to assume a position of pastoral authority. The reasons behind women's struggles with their calls to ministry are well documented: inadequate familial or institutional support for women's calls to ordained ministry, the lack of female mentors and role-models in the formation and ordination processes, and women receiving considerably fewer opportunities than men to exercise leadership roles in their local congregations.

By inviting students to lead Christian practices in the classroom, the instructors realized that we could strengthen women's confidence in their gifts for ministry. Especially for women raised in denominations in which they were excluded from leadership positions, the opportunity to lead our class in a Christian practice helped them to see that they could do likewise in their own church settings. For this reason, while it was surely exciting when students led new practices, we also were pleased that some guided us in core Christian practices, such as worship, Bible study, and prayer. When one of our students led the class in an Ignatian silent meditation on the environment, or another successfully wove traditional elements of the UMC liturgy together with alternative prayer practices into our closing worship service, we knew we were fostering in unusual ways the next generation of women and men leaders in the church — and were glad for it.

Finally, the teaching team learned a valuable pedagogical lesson about the role of Christian practices in feminist theological education. In our desire to foster excellence in Christian practices, we struggled to cede control over the practices assignment to our student leaders.

---

23. For a theological interpretation of women's struggles in authoring their calls to ordained ministry, see Joy Ann McDougall, "Weaving Garments of Grace: En-gendering a Theology of the Call to Ordained Ministry for Women Today," 149–63.

Each of us had our own ideas about how a certain woman's theology might translate into a meaningful practice for our class and was disappointed when our students' leadership didn't match our expectations. Especially when a particular week's practice had gone poorly, we found ourselves rushing to suggest possible practices for the following week so as to insure the quality of the final hour of class. While the teaching team was motivated by good intentions, we also came to understand that by directing the students in this manner, we were short-circuiting their learning process. Moreover, we were stifling the creativity and risk-taking that we explicitly wished to cultivate through the practices assignment.

Our striving for excellence in Christian practices provided the occasion for us to reconsider theologically what we meant by feminist theological education as "saving work." Simply stated, we wondered if we were placing too heavy a burden on feminist practices (as well as their practitioners) as a medium of personal and social transformation. Recall that we expected our weekly practices not only to be edifying to the participants, but also to be emancipatory praxis, that is, to transform in some concrete measure how Christians profess and practice their beliefs about God. To trade on one of Chopp's ambitious descriptions of such saving work, we expected our feminist practices "to emancipate from oppression and sin, to envision new places of flourishing, and to produce new ways of being in the world."[24] Given these high theological expectations, we realized that we risked treating Christian practices themselves as "saving works," that is, means for earning God's grace, rather than as joyful responses to God's free gift of grace.

Here we found it helpful to recall what Reformed feminist theologian Serene Jones describes as the "convictional ground" for Christian striving after "excellence of practices."[25] "As sanctified believers," Jones observes, we do well to strive for right practices, since "we are empowered to perform, in disciplined beauty, the reality of grace in our midst." At the same time, she cautions Christian congregations not to forget the "freeing power of grace," which relieves

---

24. Chopp, *Saving Work*, 102.
25. Serene Jones, "Graced Practices: Excellence and Freedom in the Christian Life," in Volf and Bass, *Practicing Theology*, 51–77, here 55.

them of the burden of achieving right practice and "sets us free to practice freely and with joy."[26] Should Christian communities overlook this freeing power of grace, they risk becoming imprisoned in a "bondage of practices" that at once saps their energies for discipleship and defeats their witness to the graciousness of God.[27]

As Christian practitioners and feminist educators, we took Jones's insights to heart. We have discovered that keeping such a theology of grace in view can help to alter our pedagogical disposition toward integrating Christian practices in the classroom. On the one hand, recalling the sanctifying power of grace strengthens our pursuit of excellence in Christian practices. It renews our commitment to attending to the material workings of grace through engaging in feminist practices in the classroom. At the same time it re-focuses our pedagogical efforts on how such practices both witness to and celebrate the transformative love of God already in our midst. On the other hand, recalling the justifying power of grace helps relativize our ambitious agenda for accomplishing concrete transformation through feminist practices in the classroom. Knowing that God's grace does not depend on the success of Christian practices encourages us to hold less tightly the reins on our students' efforts to teach Christian practices in the classroom. At the same time the justifying power of grace frees us "to practice boldly," that is, to take more risks in developing new ecclesial practices and reshaping traditional ones.[28] It frees us to participate with more imagination and vigor in the genuinely saving work of re-interpreting Christian traditions for a new day.

---

26. Ibid.
27. Ibid., 65.
28. Ibid.

# Chapter 9

# Contemporary (Pop-)Cultural Contexts and the Old Testament Classroom

*Brent A. Strawn*

*The sages, the wise men and women of our age, are often film-makers. They are the ones who are creating the root metaphors by which we seek to live. They are the ones who are providing our read on reality, our informing visions, our stories and myths.*[1]

Many theological educators, especially those involved in the professional aspects of the seminary curriculum, would agree that theological education extends beyond the seminary classroom. But one could easily go further and state that theological education *must* move beyond the walls of the seminary if it is to have any relevance or impact in the "real world" — that is, if it is to be anything more than an antiquarian exercise in arcane fields in service to ever-diminishing denominations.[2] Such movement beyond the classroom into the world can be achieved in any number of ways, including service learning, field education, or other models of professional instruction. In the present essay, I advocate a different contextualized model, one that might be conceptualized as a useful *preliminary* step: before moving *out* of the seminary classroom into the real world, the real world must first move *into* the seminary classroom.

---

1. Robert K. Johnston, *Useless Beauty: Ecclesiastes through the Lens of Contemporary Film*, 21–22.
2. Historical pursuits, arcane fields of study, and denominations of whatever kind are also, to be sure, parts of the "real world." By using this terminology, I do not mean to suggest that the seminary, theological education, or church work are something other than real; instead, I use it simply as a handy cipher for arenas, areas, and discourses that are not dominantly marked by concern with things theological.

The present essay argues for a consistent and intentional approach that brings real world issues and contemporary cultural "artifacts" (including pop-cultural examples) into the classroom. In this way, the theological classroom is prohibited from being "purely" *descriptive* or "historical" in an antiquarian sense. Instead, description, objectivity, dispassionate analysis, and the like — insofar as those are attainable (which can be debated) — are all worked out with an eye to the contemporary context and how our theological content can be *applied* or *actualized,* even if these latter tasks are temporarily delayed for the time being.

Like other models, this one can also be achieved in a number of ways if only because the public issues that can be engaged in the classroom are virtually infinite, highly complex, and often hopelessly intractable. A modest beginning, then, is recommended, even if it is not ultimately satisfying. Perhaps such a modest beginning — while not necessarily "easy" on every conceptual level — can be a classroom of sorts in and of itself wherein theologians (both students and faculty) can "practice" for the bigger game and the larger issues.

The more modest beginning or "practice exercise" involves bringing the world of contemporary (including popular) culture into the Old Testament classroom. To be sure, weightier political matters — war, economics, poverty, and so forth — and thick analyses of them are equally or more important; even so, working with these "simpler" specimens is good practice. Moreover, the most interesting of these "simple" examples are seldom far removed from the larger issues — neither, of course, is the Old Testament itself removed from them. Indeed, it is my firm belief that, especially among younger people (where the gunsights of consumer marketing and advertising are consistently leveled), media culture dominates the imagination and forms the worldview like no other source or authority.[3]

For some time, then, it has been my practice to bring specimens from contemporary media culture into my classroom, whether those are song lyrics, movie clips, poems, artistic pieces, or the like, in order

---

3. See the epigraph above from Johnston, *Useless Beauty,* 21–22. Among other things, such a sentiment raises questions regarding what is truly "authoritative" or "canonical" for contemporary people, including contemporary Christians.

to get a sense of this culture[4] and how it bears on my theological content.[5] The engagement that occurs in this process is pluriform: sometimes the *rapprochement* is mutually enriching; sometimes one side or the other comes in for critique; at still other times, the relationship might be described as one of critical solidarity.[6] What is clear, regardless, is that one major result of this practice is that it teaches students to understand that *everything is theological* — even if it appears, or patently is, *a*-theological. That is to say that, in this process, students begin to learn that they can and should perform theological analysis on absolutely everything.[7] Theological education, in this way, becomes contextualized in gross mode: the world itself — especially, for my purposes here, the world of entertainment, communication, media, advertising, and so forth — becomes a *theological* classroom no matter how far it is removed from the *seminary* classroom or content. In fact, if media culture is "canonical,"[8] then our students are never far removed from it, even when they sit in our seminary classrooms. In this light, one doesn't need to bring the external world into the classroom so much as convince the externally minded students that the theological content has bearing on what they already believe to be true and how they enact such truth.

In what follows, I discuss two examples of this kind of contextualized approach. Both come from a class on the Bible and poetry, which was supported by a Candler Contextual Education grant with the

---

4. I realize that the plural "cultures" would be more accurate in light of the complexity of contemporary North American society and the plurality of media (web, television, movie, radio, music, various print forms) with diverse clients and patrons, etc. Even so, it seems possible given the large number of national (or multi-regional) businesses and non-local media forms (esp. the web, radio, etc.) to speak in broad stokes of contemporary (popular) culture.

5. See, e.g., my contributions to Mark Roncace and Patrick Gray, eds., *Teaching the Bible: Practical Strategies for Classroom Instruction*, 15–16, 19–20, 38–39, 163–65, 175–76, 201–4, 216–18, 246–47; and Mark Roncace and Patrick Gray, eds., *Teaching the Bible through Popular Culture*, 251–322; see also Steve Delamarter, Javier Alanís, Russell Haitch, Mark Vitalis Hoffman, Arun W. Jones, and Brent A. Strawn, "Technology, Pedagogy, and Transformation in Theological Education: Five Case Studies," *Teaching Theology and Religion* 10, no. 2 (April 2007): 64–79.

6. For the language of "critical solidarity," see the discussion of the relationship of the Old and New Testaments in Ronald J. Allen and John C. Holbert, *Holy Root, Holy Branches: Christian Preaching from the Old Testament*, esp. 29–31.

7. Note the analogical and not-unrelated argument in Steven Johnson, *Everything Bad Is Good for You: How Today's Popular Culture Is Actually Making Us Smarter*.

8. See note 3 above.

express purpose of contextualizing the course in this fashion. Without the grant and the contextualization it provided, the class might easily have remained a class devoted exclusively to ancient Hebrew poetry. This is, no doubt, a worthwhile area of intellectual inquiry, but without contextualization the course could have remained an esoteric and antiquarian exercise. When contextualized, however, each class session became a roundtable discussion among a number of diverse sources. A biblical poem or two from a particular genre was set alongside numerous dialogue partners that offered contexts in which the biblical selections would be read: ancient Near Eastern poems of similar vintage or type as well as modern poems and songs that also connected with the topic at hand. In both of the class sessions discussed below it will be seen that the particular nexus provided by intersecting the biblical (theological) content with the contemporary examples shed significant light on both and suggested significant critique of certain habits and practices that are especially common in media-based popular culture. After the discussion of these two sessions, I will draw some pedagogical conclusions from the approach advocated here.

One final caveat: what is described below in rather straightforward, even linear fashion was, on the ground, less direct and much more the result of class discovery and discussion. To be sure, the materials assigned for the day had been on the syllabus for weeks and I had certain pedagogical goals and ideas already in mind. That being granted, the ideas discussed below emerged to no small degree in the process of the contextualized teaching and learning. It should also be observed that, on some of the theoretical points, much more could be said, including and especially in discussing the work of scholars who have offered similar analyses or taken up the thorny problems of sexuality and violence elsewhere outside the purview of biblical studies. The theoretical insights made below, that is, are neither completely new nor entirely original to this particular class. What *is* novel, however, is how the contextualized approach offered here spurred and facilitated those insights. Moreover, this contextualized approach permitted those insights *within a theological classroom* in a biblical studies course. This kind of rapprochement and integration is no small pedagogical achievement and suggests that an approach like the one advocated here may not only be an important preliminary step in contextualization, it may be the *ultimate contextualization* for those interested in correlating theological content with the real world.

## The Song of Songs, Pornography, and Human Decency

The first example is from a class session devoted to "The Poetry of Passion: Love Poetry." In addition to the three biblical poems from the Song of Songs that were to be assessed that day (Song 4:1–16; 5:9–16; and 8:1–7), the following readings were on the syllabus:

*Ancient Near Eastern poems:* "Egyptian Love Poems," in *The Context of Scripture*, 3 vols., ed. W. W. Hallo and K. L. Younger (Leiden: Brill, 1997–2002), 1.49–52, 125–30.

*Modern poems:* Sharon Olds, "Topography," in idem, *The Gold Cell* (New York: Knopf, 2004 [1987]), 58; Pablo Neruda, "Love," in *The Poetry of Pablo Neruda*, ed. Ilan Stavans (New York: Farrar, Straus, Giroux, 2003), 5; and idem, "Ode to a Beautiful Nude," in *The Wadsworth Anthology of Poetry*, ed. Jay Parini (Boston: Thomson Wadsworth, 2006), 438–39.

*Modern songs:* John Mayer, "Your Body Is a Wonderland" (*Heavier Things*, CD, Aware/Columbia, 2003); Michael Franks, "Innuendo" (*The Camera Never Lies*, CD, Warner Brothers, 1987); idem, "Underneath the Apple Tree" (*Tiger in the Rain*, CD, Warner Brothers, 1979); idem, "Baseball" (*One Bad Habit*, CD, Warner Brothers, 1980); Quincy Jones, "Secret Garden" (*Back on the Block*, CD, Quest/Warner Brothers, 1989).

*Secondary reading:* Robert Alter, *The Art of Biblical Poetry* (New York: Basic Books, 1985), 185–203; George Steiner, "Night Words: High Pornography and Human Privacy" in idem, *Language and Silence: Essays on Language, Literature, and the Inhuman* (New Haven: Yale University Press, 1998 [book orig.: 1970; article orig.: 1965]), 68–77.

*Recommended Reading:* Michael V. Fox, "Love and Lovers in the Love Songs," in idem, *The Song of Songs and the Ancient*

*Egyptian Love Songs* (Madison: University of Wisconsin Press, 1985), 295–331; Tod Linafelt, "Biblical Love Poetry (…and God)," *JAAR* 70 (2002): 323–45; F. W. Dobbs-Allsopp, "The Delight of Beauty and Song of Songs 4:1–7," *Interpretation* 59 (2005): 260–77.

The first two poems from the Song of Songs are known as *wasf*s — a descriptive poem-form that celebrates the body of the beloved. In the first *wasf*, the man praises the body of the woman; in the second these roles are reversed. The third poem from the Song is again the woman's voice expressing her love and desire for the man, culminating with the famous lines in 8:6–7:

> Set me as a seal upon your heart,
> > as a seal upon your arm;
> for love is strong as death,
> > passion fierce as the grave.
> Its flashes are flashes of fire,
> > a raging flame.
> Many waters cannot quench love,
> > neither can floods drown it.
> If one offered for love
> > all the wealth of one's house,
> > it would be utterly scorned. (NRSV)

Much in these three poems is devoted to sexuality, although this is done more by allusion than by explicit reference. Once one is attuned to their erotic content, which is pervasive, it is easy to find it everywhere, though that may say more about the reader than the Song itself.[9] Regardless, the nature of the Song as erotic love poetry has not kept interpreters from a long history of allegorical exegesis, even while its erotic nature challenges or chastens (nb!) the allegorical approach — at least to some degree.[10]

---

9. See Michael V. Fox, *The Song of Songs and the Ancient Egyptian Love Songs*, 298.

10. It may have been discomfort with the sexual content of the Song that gave rise to the allegorical approach. Whatever the case, see the perceptive comments of Othmar Keel, *The Song of Songs: A Continental Commentary*.

However the Song's eroticism is judged, a contextualized reading and teaching of these poems reveals that it is of a particular, understated sort. While it is certainly possible to find sexuality everywhere in the Song, it is far from certain that it actually *is* everywhere, even if one grants the fluidity and openness of the poetic speech *qua* poetry. Moreover, as Michael V. Fox points out, even though "sexual desire pervades the songs, and sexual pleasure is happily widespread in them.... their eroticism is not concentrated where commentators most often seek it: in specific allusions to genitalia and coitus."[11] The modern poems and songs assigned for the class session reinforce this point on a number of levels. Take, for instance, Pablo Neruda's "Ode to a Beautiful Nude," which begins

> With a chaste heart,
> with pure eyes,
> I celebrate your beauty.[12]

He proceeds to describe the "beautiful nude" in poetic detail — beginning with her feet. Lest one accuse Neruda of having a foot fetish, he proceeds from the feet to the ears (!) before moving to other parts of the woman's body: breasts, eyelids, shoulders, spinal line, and other regions, replete with allusive and erotic metaphors not unlike those found in the Song of Songs, until he comes to the final line: "The moon lives in the lining of your skin."[13] Comparing the Song with Neruda's poem reveals a poetic technique: reticence.[14] Poems — good ones, anyway — do not tell us too much; they don't give it all away. A beautiful nude "dressed" in poetry, as it were, turns out to be more seductive than one starkly naked, shown in "full frontal nudity." By means of metaphor, reticence, and other poetic devices, Neruda demonstrates that he does in fact have a chaste heart and pure eyes and that it is precisely these organs that enable him to celebrate the lover's beauty, nude as it may be (and, in truth, actually is).

---

11. Fox, *The Song of Songs*, 298.
12. Pablo Neruda, "Ode to a Beautiful Nude," in Jay Parini, ed., *The Wadsworth Anthology of Poetry*, 438.
13. Ibid., 439.
14. See James Longenbach, *The Resistance to Poetry*; also Mary Kinzie, *A Poet's Guide to Poetry*, passim, esp. 142–86.

Similar devices are at work in the other compositions — the Egyptian love songs, which may bear a close relationship with the Song of Songs;[15] Sharon Olds's "Topography," which maps two lovers' bodies onto each other like a map folded along the centerline of the Continental United States ("my / New Orleans deep in your Texas, your Idaho / bright on my Great Lakes, my Kansas / burning against your Kansas your Kansas / burning against my Kansas");[16] Michael Franks's songs, which are delights of metaphor and innuendo; and, with less poetic skill, but similar allusiveness and understatement, the songs by John Mayer and Quincy Jones. The contextualization of the Song of Songs created by comparison with these various compositions reveals that sexuality can be celebrated, even enhanced and made more powerful, by allusive poetry which traffics in metaphor that includes restatement and understatement.

Extending beyond the classroom, it might be noted that these elements are exactly what do *not* pass for sexuality and the erotic in most media contexts. Instead, we seem to be offered two polarized options: a kind of flight from the sexual/erotic or an addiction to it. The former is perhaps manifested in "family safe" media of various types, by G-rated animated movies, and by studious — even puritanical — avoidance of sexual topics, or, possibly paradigmatically, by the allegorical interpretation of the Song of Songs itself as being about almost everything *but* eroticism. The second option, addiction to the sexual/erotic, is nowhere more clearly manifested than in the massive juggernaut that is the porn industry, which brings in $8–10 billion annually from U.S. Americans alone.[17] But it is not just pornography in its full-blown form that is cause for concern; one thinks also of the "pornographication" of general culture — manifested in many different ways[18] — such that even if one is watching a "family safe" television show, one must remain alert lest one's small children get exposed to inappropriate content during the thirty-second commercial breaks.

---

15. See Fox, *The Song of Songs.*
16. Sharon Olds, "Topography," in idem, *The Gold Cell,* 58.
17. Statistics come from the Christian anti-porn website, *xxxchurch.com* (accessed January 22, 2007).
18. E.g., much top-40 radio, especially among certain hip hop and rap artists.

With attention to these broader cultural contexts, the poetics of
the Song of Songs and the other love poetry surveyed offers an alternative — a *media via* between a prudish Puritanism on the one
hand, and pornography on the other. It says, first, that one need not
be a sex addict to celebrate and delight in the erotic and the sexual.
Conceding these latter realms solely to the purview of the pornogra-
pher is, in fact, a large part of the problem. Similarly, the presence
of the Song of Songs in the canon of Scripture (and similar themes in
the "canon" of experience) indicates that puritanical flight from the
sexual is neither a reasonable nor a necessary solution. One can, in
truth, celebrate the beauty of a nude with "pure eyes" and "a chaste
heart" (Neruda).

Second and even more importantly, however, the poetics of the
Song of Songs, contextualized as above, indicates that there can be
true, real, beautiful — and erotic — sexuality, without the profound
problems and injustices associated with the porn industry.[19] In no
small part, the "prophylactic" offered by the poetics of the love
poetry discussed here is that they do contain real sexuality. *Something
really happens* down in that garden! There is a point of "crescendo,"
which "makes the dialogue all real / not just innuendo" — as Michael
Franks sings ("Innuendo"). And yet the Song of Songs knows that
love — *all* love, but even and especially erotic love — is risky, dan-
gerous.[20] It is as strong as death (Song 8:6) — one ought not rouse
love before its time (Song 2:7; 3:5; 8:4). Moreover, the real sexuality
in the love poetry is *not* pornographic, it does not tell too much, it
doesn't give it all away, it is not indecent, nor is it unjust — it is not
an offense against human decency and privacy.

At this point George Steiner's withering critique of pornography is
incisive. "Where everything can be said with a shout, less and less can

---

19. A few examples from many: a 1986 study of sexually abused women revealed that
21 percent of these knew that the perpetrator of the abuse was heavily into pornography; it
is believed that 70 percent of women involved in pornography are survivors of incest or child
sexual abuse; 30 percent of unsolicited emails contain pornographic content; 51 percent of
pastors admit that looking at Internet pornography is their biggest temptation. This is not
to mention the horrible statistics regarding "kiddie porn," which is illegal worldwide. For
example, 20 percent of all Internet pornography involves children; more than twenty thousand
images of child pornography are posted on the Internet every week; more than half of all illegal
sites are hosted in the United States (source: *www.xxxchurch.com*).

20. See esp. Tod Linafelt, "Biblical Love Poetry (... and God)," 323–45.

be said in a low voice," he writes.[21] He argues that pornographers do not respect human freedom and there is thus a deep connection between the lack (and deprivation) of privacy, on the one hand (which he associates with pornography[22]) and dehumanization, on the other (which he associates with totalitarian regimes). It is no coincidence, Steiner argues, that there is a marked similarity with regard to what pornographers and S.S. prison guards in World War II make human beings do with their bodies.[23] In our own time, the parallel with the Abu Grab (Ghraib) prison scandal in Iraq is profoundly disturbing.

> There may be deeper affinities than we as yet understand between the "total freedom" of the uncensored erotic imagination and the total freedom of the sadist. That these two freedoms have emerged in close historical proximity may not be coincidence. Both are exercised at the expense of someone else's humanity, of someone else's most precious right — the right to a private life of feeling.[24]

In the place of such unjust practices, Steiner advocates a return to literary devices that are also at work in the Song of Songs: "Respect for the reader signifies that the poet or novelist invites the consciousness of the reader to collaborate with his own in the act of presentment. He does not tell all because his work is not a primer for children or the retarded."[25] Unfortunately, what we now have, Steiner believes — and he wrote his essay in 1965 (!) — is "a massive onslaught on human privacy...being pressed by the very conditions of an urban mass-technocracy."[26] Contrary to anticensorship, first-amendment rhetoric, such a situation actually robs us of freedom:

---

21. George Steiner, "Night Words: High Pornography and Human Privacy" in idem, *Language and Silence: Essays on Language, Literature, and the Inhuman*, 68. Steiner's concern is pornographic *literature*, but it is still broadly applicable. See also the related critiques of Bruce F. Kawin, *Telling It Again and Again: Repetition in Literature and Film*, 65–70; and Albert Manguel, *Into the Looking-Glass Wood: Essays on Books, Reading, and the World*, 85–105.

22. Steiner, "Night Words," 75: "The very opposite of freedom is cliché, and nothing is less free, more inert with convention and hollow brutality, than a row of four-letter words."

23. Ibid., 68.

24. Ibid., 76.

25. Ibid., 75.

26. Ibid., 76.

My true quarrel...is that these books leave a man less free, less himself, than they found him; that they leave language poorer, less endowed with a capacity for fresh discrimination and excitement. It is not a new freedom that they bring, but a new servitude. In the name of human privacy, enough![27]

And Steiner's quarrel is even more substantive when we add images, movies, and websites to his category of "literature," and when we include the persons involved in producing such products, not just those who "read" them.

Steiner points out that in contrast to this parading and shouting of the sexual and the erotic,

[s]exual relations are, or should be, one of the citadels of privacy, the nightplace where we must be allowed to gather the splintered, harried elements of our consciousness to some kind of inviolate order and repose. It is in sexual experience that...we may find for ourselves, through imperfect striving and repeated failure, the words, the gestures, the mental images which set the blood to racing. In that dark and wonder ever renewed both the fumblings and the light must be our own.[28]

But it is precisely "this last, vital privacy" that pornographers subvert and pervert. "[T]hey do our imagining for us. They take away the words that were of the night and shout them over the rooftops, making them hollow."[29] To combat this tendency, Steiner reminds us that "much of Western poetry and fiction has been a school to the imagination, an exercise in making one's awareness more exact, more humane."[30] In the cases of sexuality, eroticism, love, and pornography, this is no simple literary matter but a pressing issue that has profound ethical significance. In addition to what has already been stated, we might note that several writers have stressed that beauty suggests categories (and ethics) of justice and purity.[31] It is no

---

27. Ibid., 77; see also 75. Given the fact that most consumers of pornography are male, the non-inclusive language is probably apropos.
28. Ibid., 76–77.
29. Ibid., 77.
30. Ibid.
31. See Elaine Scarry, *On Beauty and Being Just;* and F. W. Dobbs-Allsopp, "The Delight of Beauty and Song of Songs 4:1–7," 260–77.

coincidence, then, that Olds's poem, "Topography," concludes the merging of the lovers' mapped bodies on a note of justice

> sealing us together,
> all our cities twin cities,
> all our states united, one
> nation, indivisible, with liberty and justice for all.[32]

Nor is it surprising that Neruda's poem, "Love," speaks of feeling his beloved in his veins, watching her pass by, and that he hopes to so "emerge in the stanza — cleansed of all evil."[33]

To summarize: contextualizing the Song of Songs in the way advocated here not only helps one understand the biblical text better; it also demonstrates how these ancient love poems have a compelling and critical word for the way sexuality is discussed and practiced in the "real world." In the final analysis, the Song of Songs is not just about *love*, including *sexual love*; it is also about *ethics*, including *sexual ethics*.

## *Lamentations, Violence, and Human Dignity*

If Susan Sontag is correct, and "[w]hat pornography is really about, ultimately, isn't sex but death,"[34] then there is a close connection between the first case study and the second. The proximity of the two subjects will be further borne out below. The second example of cultural contextualization is from the first of two class sessions devoted to "Deathly Poetry." This session dealt with the Book of Lamentations with primary attention to Lamentations 1. In addition to the biblical poem, the following readings were on the syllabus:

> *Ancient Near Eastern poems:* "Lamentation over the Destruction of Sumer and Ur," in *The Context of Scripture*, 3 vols., ed. W. W. Hallo and K. L. Younger (Leiden: Brill, 1997–2002), 1.166: 535–39.

---

32. Olds, "Topography," 58.
33. Pablo Neruda, "Love," in *The Poetry of Pablo Neruda*, ed. Ilan Stavans, 5.
34. Cited in Manguel, *Into the Looking-Glass Wood*, 99; see further 85–105. The connection between sex and death is, of course, longstanding. Compare *la petite mort*.

*Modern poems:* D. H. Lawrence, "The Hills," in *The Complete Poems of D. H. Lawrence*, 2 vols., ed. Vivian de Sola Pinto and Warren Roberts (New York: Viking, 1964), 2:660; Reed Whittemore, "Psalm," in *Good Poems*, ed. Garrison Keillor (New York: Penguin, 2002), 13; Osip Mandelstam, "I was washing outside in the darkness," in *Against Forgetting: Twentieth-Century Poetry of Witness*, ed. Carolyn Forche (New York: W. W. Norton, 1993), 124; Wislawa Szymborska, "Hunger Camp at Jaslo," in *Against Forgetting: Twentieth-Century Poetry of Witness*, ed. Carolyn Forche (New York: W. W. Norton, 1993), 459–60; Edward Bond, "How We See," in *Holocaust Poetry*, ed. Hilda Schiff (New York: St. Martin's, 1995), 156.

*Modern song:* Sufjan Stevens, "Casimir Pulaski Day" (*Illinoise*, CD, Asthmatic Kitty Records, 2005).

*Secondary reading:* Jay Parini, ed., *The Wadsworth Anthology of Poetry* (Boston: Thomson Wadsworth, 2006), 128–31.

Lamentations 1 is a carefully constructed piece of Hebrew poetry. Within a larger framework provided by an alphabetic acrostic structure,[35] the poem reveals similar techniques and strategies to what was seen in the love poetry discussed above. The content, of course, is radically changed, however. The poem begins with the famous words:

> Alas!
> Lonely sits the city
> Once great with people!
> She that was great among nations
> Is become like a widow;
> The princess among states
> Is become a thrall. (Lam 1:1; NJPSV)

This plaintive opening signals what the book is all about: the destruction of Jerusalem by the Babylonians in 596/586 B.C.E. and the aftermath that followed. As such, the book is full of disturbing images of starving people, broken bodies, cannibalism, misery, and pain the

---

35. This means that each verse begins with a successive letter of the Hebrew alphabet — making it about grief from "A to Z," as it were.

like of which can only be imagined in comparably extreme scenarios of war, occupation, and poverty.

The poet of Lamentations 1 makes these points in an elusive way, using strategies of concealment-amid-revelation and revelation-amid-concealment similar to those that were found in the love poetry of the Song of Songs. The devastation is *imaged,* to be sure — and in disturbingly vivid ways (e.g., empty gates, v. 4; infants taken captive, v. 5; people bartered for food, v. 11) — but is not described in unnecessary and over-the-top gore à la the latest blood-and-guts horror movie. In fact, by means of a major poetic device — personification, which is initiated already in v. 1 and which takes a dramatic turn in v. 9 — the poet of Lamentations 1 achieves and maintains something that the horror genre seems to dispense with entirely, namely, *the dignity of the victim.*

Destroyed Jerusalem is personified in Lamentations 1:1 as a woman of royal lineage, but she is also called "daughter" and "maiden" and "widow" — all of which invite affection and/or sympathy.[36] Personification functions to make what could be seen dispassionately, at a distance — the destruction of a city — far more immediate, concrete, and engaging. As F. W. Dobbs-Allsopp has written: it "ups the emotional ante" and "gives authenticity and sharpness to the city's plight by individuating the experience."[37] Cities can be rebuilt, after all, but bodies tend to keep their scars. Similarly, some of the images used to describe Jerusalem's personified suffering bear notable resemblances to passages that are found in the prophets which describe punishment using sexual imagery. The difference, in Lamentations 1, is that the personification functions to portray such punishments *from the perspective of the victim.* This promotes sympathy in the reader who must engage the victim as a human being, not simply as a nameless, numbered prisoner facing their horrific punishment.[38] Throughout the chapter, in these various ways, the fate that Jerusalem has faced (and

---

36. Here and throughout the comments on Lamentations 1 below, I am heavily indebted to F. W. Dobbs-Allsopp's excellent commentary (*Lamentations*), which is easily the best poetic analysis of Lamentations to appear in print.

37. Ibid., 52.

38. See ibid., 64–65.

continues to face) is described in sufficient, but not exhaustive, detail. Clearly there is great suffering here, but it is presented in elusive fashion and that to great effect.[39]

There is an important development in the personification that begins in v. 9: personified Zion is no longer just discussed in third person discourse; she now speaks in the first person (see also vv. 11b–16, 18–22). When she does so, she gives voice to her suffering and, "in especially dark language," identifies her chief tormenter: God.[40] When the poem is read (and this is even clearer when it is read aloud), this shift to first-person discourse functions to collapse the distance between the speaking subject that is Zion and the reading subject (i.a., the reader). "The use of the first-person voice draws readers into the poem, makes them identify with the speaker, and invites them to experience vicariously the suffering and affliction that the poem figures."[41] Moreover, the "dark language" makes it difficult for us (or God) to ignore and justify the suffering that is discussed.[42] To be sure, it is clear from the content of Lamentations that sin is part of the problem — sin and culpability for sin is a viable and employed explanation for the destruction that has happened; there is, in a word, *confession* in the Book of Lamentations (see, e.g., 1:18, 20, 22). But there is also "subtle and oblique" resistance to an overly simplistic "sin caused this" justification for Zion's suffering.[43] That resistance is accomplished, in part, by the fact that the poem lays the cause of Jerusalem's plight not solely at the city's door, but also at God's door (1:12–15, 17, 22) and at the enemies' door (e.g., 1:16, 19, 21–22). "In this way ... the poem is able to give credence to both realities, the reality of sin and the reality of suffering, while at the same time insisting that these realities must be considered and weighed together."[44]

Whatever the case, the first-person speaking subject of personified Zion (and, more broadly, the suffering community/poet responsible for the Book of Lamentations) is a sign of hope — slim though it may be. The city is forsaken and desolate ... but not yet deceased,

---

39. Ibid., 67.
40. Ibid., 50; see also 72.
41. Ibid., 50.
42. Ibid., 72.
43. Ibid., 61.
44. Ibid.

not yet completely finished. Even groaning, that is, witnesses to a presence "that refuses to be silenced."[45] Still further, in no small way, Lamentations 1 indicates that this movement from silence to speech is *transformative*: "If we can only name our pain and hurt and find a language that can figure it, then we may ultimately dare to hope and to endure."[46] And it may well be the case that such hope and endurance is facilitated and made possible by the poet's "ability to find a vocabulary that is able to figure the immensity and intensity of the community's suffering in a way that [yet] remains respectful of those who have suffered."[47]

Again, a large number of these observations also hold true for the other poems that were assigned for class discussion; indeed, these other compositions help to bring these poetic and hermeneutical observations into even sharper relief. D. H. Lawrence's "The Hills," for example, in its dark play off of Psalm 121, identifies darkness and blindness (=grief and lament?) as loci for strength:

> I lift up mine eyes unto the hills
> and there they are, but no strength
> comes from them to me.
>
> Only from darkness
> and ceasing to see
> strength comes.[48]

Similarly, Reed Whittemore's "Psalm" speaks of the "dark images of our Lord" — images such as:

> The Lord feeds some of His prisoners better than others.
> It could be said of Him that He is not a just god but an
>      indifferent god
>
> . . .

---

45. Ibid., 74.
46. Ibid., 74–75.
47. Ibid., 75.
48. D. H. Lawrence, "The Hills," in *The Complete Poems of D. H. Lawrence,* ed. Vivian de Sola Pinto and Warren Roberts, 2:660. See also Karl A. Plank, "Ascent to Darker Hills: Psalm 121 and Its Poetic Revision," 152–67, esp. 160–61.

> That he maketh the poor poorer but is otherwise
>     undependable.[49]

And yet, despite all that, this Lord is still "ours" and we "rush back
into the safer fold, impressed by His care for us."[50] Given Whittemore's dark images, one might well wonder how safe that fold is, but
it is revealed as at least relatively so given the alternative — "praying
not unto Him / But ourselves. / But when we do that we find that indeed we are truly lost."[51] Personified Zion finds the same to be true in
the Book of Lamentations, where, despite identifying the Lord as her
enemy (e.g., 2:4–5), she continues to call upon the Lord and beseech
her God (e.g., 1:9, 20–22).

Like Whittemore, Edward Bond's poem writes us into its own grief.
For his part, Whittemore makes his readers one of the "we" who end
up walking with God and one of the "we" who continue to claim
God as "our Lord." For his part, Bond writes "us" into the story of
the Holocaust:

> After Treblinka
> And the *spezialkommando*
> Who tore a child with bare hands
> Before its mother in Warsaw
> We see differently.[52]

The poetic "we" are those who stood in Warsaw, after Treblinka,
and the unspeakable act of the *spezialkommando* (who is, it should
be noted, *de*-personified). But the "we" also includes those who now
read Bond's poem. "We" are they. We, too, see differently, including
seeing "racist slogans chalked on walls differently / We see walls differently."[53] When "they" who have witnessed and experienced such
horrors are now "we," there is no possibility of distancing ourselves
from the victims, nor can we view their (our!) suffering dispassionately, objectively, as if it were not of import to us. It is, instead,

---

49. Reed Whittemore, "Psalm," in *Good Poems*, ed. Garrison Keillor, 13.
50. Ibid.
51. Ibid. The song by Sufjan Stevens has similar motifs; the "safer fold" is less clearly signaled
though it may be implied by and present in the bright musical setting that contrasts with the
sober content of a girl diagnosed with bone cancer.
52. Edward Bond, "How We See," in *Holocaust Poetry*, ed. Hilda Schiff, 156.
53. Ibid.

of *profound* *import* to us because it is *about us.* Such is the power of personification and first-person poetic discourse in the context of reading.

Perhaps these considerations speak yet again to Theodor Adorno's oft-quoted and oft-contested dictum that it is barbaric to write poetry after Auschwitz.[54] In fact, to write poetry after Auschwitz may be the farthest thing from barbaric one can imagine: poetry about suffering may be exceedingly and profoundly *humane.* Poetry of witness, like that concerning the Shoah, plays an important role here,[55] but so does "deathly poetry" like Lamentations 1, which also concerns a Shoah of a sort. In each case, what one finds is poetry that is about real suffering but not in a blood-and-guts, slash horror show, sadistic sort of way; instead, one finds a poetry that traffics in images that reveal real pain all the while engaging the imagination and not telling too much.[56] One also finds a poetry that gives transformative voice to suffering, permitting the victim to speak, permitting — even requiring — the listener to feel addressed by and identify with those in pain and grief. Such poetry may prove a salve to the sufferer and a compulsion to compassion for the reader/listener/observer.[57]

Such moves are arguably facilitated by poetry better than they are in prose, and we have already witnessed the power of understatement, metaphor, and reticence in the love poetry discussed above where they suggested a kind of sexual ethic — one at profound odds with much of what passes for love and sex in popular media culture. If these poetic devices — underscored by contextualized analysis and

---

54. See Berel Lang and Aron Appelfeld, *Writing and the Holocaust,* 179.

55. So Bond's poem. See also Wislawa Szymborska, "Hunger Camp at Jaslo," in *Against Forgetting: Twentieth-Century Poetry of Witness,* ed. Carolyn Forche (New York: W. W. Norton, 1993), 459–60: "Write it. Write. In ordinary ink / on ordinary paper: they were given no food, / they all died of hunger. 'All. How many? / It's a big meadow. How much grass / for each one?' Write: I don't know."

56. Note, e.g., Osip Mandelstam's ominous lines: "I was washing outside in the darkness, / the sky burning with rough stars, / and the starlight, salt on an axe-blade. / The cold overflows the barrel" ("I was washing outside in the darkness," in *Against Forgetting: Twentieth-Century Poetry of Witness,* ed. Carolyn Forche [New York: W. W. Norton, 1993], 124).

57. One might note that Lawrence's poem appeared in a collection entitled *More Pansies,* which is related to an earlier collection called simply *Pansies.* In the introduction to the earlier book, he explained the title: "Or, if you will have the other derivation of pansy, from *panser,* to dress or soothe a wound; these are my tender administrations to the mental and emotional wounds we suffer from. Or you can have heartsease if you like, since the modern heart could certainly do with it" (Lawrence, *The Complete Poems,* 1:417). See Plank, "Ascent to Darker Hills," 157 and n. 23.

examples — also hold true for love and sex, then it should come as
no surprise that they also apply to contemporary media presentations of violence, hurt, and suffering. One thinks, for example, of the
6:00 p.m. news where an at best thinly edited description of the latest
gruesome homicide is recounted in 10 seconds (or less) before the anchor smilingly turns to the upcoming weather forecast. How is that
*news?* How is the dignity of the brutalized victim (pre)served by such
"news"? When one turns to consider the role of violence in entertainment media, the problem is exacerbated. Witness the rise (and
dominance) of law/murder television dramas that are increasingly
grisly — e.g., the sequence of shows (not just one) concerning crime
scene investigation (C.S.I.) in various major U.S. cities — but where
the victims of the crime are almost entirely backdrop for the story
of the victimizer or, even more disturbingly, backdrop for the sexy
detectives who work out their love relationships and work problems
in the midst of a scene still bloody from murder. Quite apart from
the question of whether (and how) we should (and could) view such
shows as "entertainment" is the subject of how such shows present
suffering and how their blatant inattention to the victim and the victim's dignity (we *see* each victim's corpse in its ghastly, depersonalized
state; we even see *inside* their bodies) actually constitutes further violence and victimization against the deceased. And, lest one counter
that those are just shows "for fun" (!), we might turn to the genre
of reality television or shock television (or radio) talk shows where
people's pains, hurts, failures, sufferings, and grief are all recorded,
shot in tight close-up, replayed in slow motion, shouted from the
roof top (where the satellite receiver sits), and "entertainized." The
result is a spectacle not unlike the gladiator games of ancient Rome —
the "spectacle-ization" of the aggrieved. Even if the grief is relatively
minor, from which the sufferer can expect to recover in a short time
with little residual effect, the "spectacle-ized"process has added another issue to the sufferer's pain, which may last much longer than the
original grief: shame. And this is because — in no small measure —
the poetics of reticence have been completely eschewed. There is no
more concealment, no more metaphor, no more allusion and elusion;
only close-ups, parade, spectacle.

To sum up: the poetics of Lamentations 1, contextualized with comparable examples from other sources, reveals that understatement, allusion, imagistic language, and the like play an important role vis-à-vis suffering. On the one hand, they indicate that real suffering is taking place or has already transpired. The city truly does sit lonely, she really has become a widow (Lam. 1:1). The poetic devices give voice to this suffering. It is not censored or made taboo.[58] But the poetry gives voice to suffering in a *restrained way* — one that preserves *human dignity,* not unlike how the poetics of love poetry preserve *human decency.* In both cases, poetry, at its best in multiple contexts, casts a different light on contemporary practices, ethics, even entertainment.

## *Conclusions*

The two case studies presented above have revealed that the kind of contextualized approach advocated here can be evocative, generative, constructive, and critical. While the different materials selected for comparison with the biblical (theological) content were largely similar and reinforcing, they nevertheless cast significant light on the biblical poems. The devices at work in the Song of Songs and Lamentations, that is, are present in those texts regardless of whether or not one compares them with other compositions. But the contextualization created by the other compositions brings these devices into sharp relief and shows that the issues at work in the biblical text are still lively for the "real world."[59] The real world also knows of these issues and subjects; still more importantly, the various "artifacts" — both ancient and modern, biblical and non-biblical — cast light on contemporary practices and (re)presentations, which could benefit these latter and help make life more decent, more humane, more dignified.

---

58. For the deleterious effects of censoring death, see the fascinating essay by Geoffrey Gorer, "The Pornography of Death," in idem, *Death, Grief, and Mourning,* 192–99.

59. Plank's comments on his own method, derived largely from intertextual theory and midrash, are not unrelated: "The midrashic revision does not change the text itself, but makes manifest features of it that would remain hidden if not evoked by the framing presence of the intertext.... Intertextual midrash ... seeks to exploit possibilities of textual interpretation and make a reader aware of certain potential meanings in a text" ("Ascent to Darker Hills," 155, 161).

How is such a process distinctively *theological?* For one, it is theological insofar as it correlates theological (biblical) content with the present context. In so doing, it demonstrates that subjects from the contemporary setting can be assessed — positively *and* negatively — via the tools and texts of theology and Scripture. Despite the fact that the above examples showed a (mostly) positive correlation between the biblical texts and the other compositions, they also revealed that these were united in a negative critique of certain habits and practices in contemporary media culture. So, again, the relationship between the theological content, the contextualized examples, and the contemporary setting is not unidirectional but manifold and pluriform.[60] Whatever the case, this contextualization process reveals that all subjects can be analyzed theologically, all subjects are "theologized," as it were — they are made potential objects for theological reflection, no matter how far they "live" from the seminary classroom. Indeed, no small result of this type of contextualization approach is that we see once again that "theology" can be broadly written so as to encompass entities far beyond actual speech about God, and can include the interconnection of discourse about God and God's ways with (any and all) discourse about the non-God world.

To conclude: the goal to extend theological education beyond the classroom can be achieved in many different ways. But the approach I have presented here reverses the direction of that extension: first, the world *beyond* the classroom is brought *into* the classroom. And yet this reversal of direction is at best temporary: before the class time has expired, the students have returned — at least conceptually — to the world beyond the classroom, only now they are armed with

---

60. One may perhaps describe this process of comparison between the biblical/theological material and the modern data as one of critical correlation. It begins, regardless, with juxtaposition — setting the two data sets out next to each other. Only then can comparison take place. It is important to stress that the juxtaposition and comparison need not be unfairly stacked. The materials for the Bible and Poetry class presented here were selected well in advance before the lecture content was written or finalized. The heat and light that resulted from the juxtaposition and comparison, that is, were not pre-fabricated but emerged as a delightful serendipity and — more accurately — as a result of the juxtaposition and comparison practice itself. In all cases, this type of comparison — knowing when to compare and what to compare — is something of an art, perhaps "more like grasping a proverb, catching an allusion, seeing a joke — or...reading a poem" than it is a mechanical process (see Clifford Geertz, "'From the Native's Point of View': On the Nature of Anthropological Understanding," in idem, *Local Knowledge: Further Essays in Interpretive Anthropology,* 70).

new theological tools with which to evaluate and engage that world. What could possibly be more contextual than the world wherein we live, move, and have our being? For Christians, of course, that world is never just the world of contemporary culture, dominated by media, with its instruments of discourse and rhetoric; it is also *God's world,* since "we live and move and have our being" (Acts 17:28) in God.[61] In this contextualization process, theological education becomes *public* theology, *public* policy, *public* poetry — but public theology, policy, and poetry that knows something of, is built on, and even predicated upon, knowledge of the public *reality.* "Contextual Education" is, therefore, never to be simplistically equated with "service learning" but should include living in and thinking about the real world with the real tools of theology constantly in hand and constantly in mind. Both entities — the world and the tools of theology — will be enriched and enhanced in the process.[62]

---

61. It is quite noteworthy for the purposes of this essay to observe that some scholars believe that the Acts text may be a quotation from the sixth century B.C.E. philosopher-poet Epimenides, who was obviously *not* a Christian.

62. I would like to thank Katie Heffelfinger (Teaching Associate) and Melissa Range (Poet-in-Residence), who co-taught the Bible and Poetry course with me. I am also indebted to Steve Kraftchick and Robert Williamson Jr. for reading and commenting on an earlier version of this essay.

# Chapter 10

# Exegesis as an Ecclesial Practice

*Luke Timothy Johnson*

The title of this essay is also the stated goal of my course called New Testament Interpretation. I have taught it for fourteen years at Candler School of Theology as a two-semester course for second-year master of divinity students. For six years I taught a version of the same course at Yale Divinity School, and for ten years another version to undergraduates at Indiana University. Over these thirty years I have shaped a pedagogy that fits my (developing) vision of biblical exegesis as a practice of the church. I have come — by fits and starts — to the understanding that if it is the church as church that interprets Scripture, and if the church as a community of readers is itself always diverse and culturally conditioned, then the exegesis of the New Testament is inevitably and irreducibly contextual as well.

I use first-person narrative here because this is not a grand theoretical statement but the story of one teacher's struggle, which is by no means finished, and because an account of my fits and starts may offer some encouragement to others engaged in the same struggle to shape a mode of theological discourse that at once has scholarly integrity and ecclesial pertinence. I speak in the first person as well because the struggle I recount is also inevitably contextualized by the particular circumstances of my life and especially my experience of teaching this subject to these students across the last three decades in the United States of America.

The effort to locate New Testament interpretation within the life of the church encounters resistance at times from deeply entrenched positions within the guild of New Testament scholars. Bible scholars in general and New Testament scholars in particular often consider themselves critical gatekeepers of revelation for the rest of the faculty and curriculum. New Testament scholarship can be insular and resistant to change. Standard practices of teaching New Testament, dominated over the past century by the historical-critical method, often leave students with the choice between the ways they have read Scripture in the church and the ways in which it is read in the academy.[1]

This essay recounts the stages through which I came to an alternative vision of how the New Testament should be read, and therefore also, how it should be taught.

## *The Birth of Awareness*

I first encountered the standard way of teaching New Testament when I was a Ph.D. student at Yale University and served as a teaching assistant at Yale Divinity School. I came to this task, though, with a different background than many of the other students. First, I was not only Roman Catholic but was still a Benedictine monk. This meant I had a strong sense of community and of the reading of Scripture as a transformative practice, both in the Divine Office and in *Lectio Divina*. Second, I was a participant-observer in the Catholic charismatic movement, in which powerful religious experiences "opened the Scriptures" in ways many Catholics had not previously known. Third, I had already grown disenchanted with the "historical method," because in the fierce battles over liturgical reform in the monastery following Vatican II, those of us who were "right" historically were quite willing to disregard the religious experience of our brothers in the monastery, and on the basis of better historical knowledge, destroy delicate and longstanding practices of piety.

My first exposure to the way exegesis was taught at Yale Divinity School between 1971 and 1975 was disconcerting. New Testament Introduction was a year-long course based entirely in lectures and weekly discussions led by teaching assistants. The approach was

---

1. For further discussion, see L. T. Johnson, *The Real Jesus: The Misguided Quest for the Historical Jesus and the Truth of the Traditional Gospels,* 57–80, and with William S. Kurz, *The Future of Catholic Biblical Scholarship: A Constructive Conversation,* 3–34.

purely historical-critical: introduction meant finding out what the text meant in its original context as scholarship could reconstruct it. The discussions took up topics covered in the lectures. One exegesis paper was assigned each semester. The exegesis paper was basically a research paper. Students were to read commentaries and if possible scholarly articles or monographs to find the correct reading of the New Testament passage. After establishing the text, discussing its language and its critical issues, and summarizing the best scholarly positions with regard to its meaning, students would then add, at the end, a paragraph "applying" the passage to the present day, usually through some homiletical observation.

Some of the problems in this pedagogy were obvious to me from the first, and others took longer for me to appreciate. The most obvious problem is that writing two papers a year is not enough to learn even an individualistic practice: the emphasis inevitably was put on product rather than process. Excellent students performed superbly, poor students performed miserably, but no one learned skills through a process of trial and feedback. It was also clear that the research model made exegesis a scholarship of the academy rather than the church. It did not create powerful and imaginative readers with confidence in their own judgment, but researchers who gave authority to commentaries and saw themselves simply as gatherers and reporters of expert opinions. The "go to the commentaries" approach also perpetuated the top-down model of theological education: Scripture is obscure, and its true meaning is available only to the experts. The pastor-to-be cannot possibly challenge such learning or find an independent reading. There is only one right meaning, and it must be derived from the experts. The pastor is thereby implicitly taught to depend on commentaries for preaching and teaching rather than to become a powerful interpreter. Finally, the form of the paper, with all the serious work being given to "the meaning of the text" and only a paragraph assigned to "today's meaning" perpetuated two interrelated notions: that the analysis of texts is hard, but the analysis of life is easy; and the traffic in theology moves only one way, from the Bible to life, and never from life to the text.

## *More Awareness, First Steps*

When I began teaching New Testament Introduction as an assistant professor at Yale Divinity School (at first, team-teaching with Carl Holladay), I slowly introduced changes. Rather than a single long paper each semester, I required two short, five-page papers each semester. Four papers is still not enough to form a practice, but it is a start, especially since students received immediate feedback from teaching assistants and end-of-semester feedback from me. More significant, students were forbidden to use commentaries or other scholarly publications. I wanted to see their minds at work on the text. The shift was from the gathering of information to the act of interpretation. Without quite realizing it, I was started on the path toward contextualization, for I made the authority of the reader a real factor in the process and encouraged the reader to exercise that authority rather than depend on the authority of the experts.

My instructions concerning papers were not about research techniques, but on the basics of good reading (analysis of sentences, immediate and remote contexts) and on the basic tools for all responsible interpretation (use of the synopsis, concordance). Remarkably, the papers did not decline in quality and were, for the most part, no less responsible than in the earlier system; indeed, students were able to exercise their intelligence in more creative ways, and I began to learn new things from student work. I eliminated entirely the paragraph devoted to application, hoping thereby to suggest that the exegesis of life requires at least as much attention as the exegesis of texts.

Equally significant to my growth in awareness while at Yale Divinity School (YDS) was my participation for six years in a field-based course in Pastoral Care and Counseling in the Parish with Lucia Ewing (which confirmed my sense of the importance of personal narratives as revelatory), and the many hours I spent in the office listening to students — it took me a while to shift from priest to professor. Listening to students in such an intensive fashion made me acutely aware of the gap between our New Testament pedagogy, with its assumptions, and their situation. In my last two years at YDS, I developed a course called "Christian Existence as Life in the Spirit," which I offered first as a pilot (for three students) and then to the general population. This course based itself squarely on the personal narratives of students, analyzed repeatedly from the perspective of different theological concepts. In the experimental version, everything could be done orally, and the effect was powerfully transforming.

When I offered the course to the student body at large, however, some sixty students registered! I had to scramble to find a way of capturing the intense effect of the pilot course for a large class. Out of necessity, I began to use small group work in a way I had not before. In large class presentations, I would talk about the theological concepts. Students would then work intensely at those concepts in groups of three. Then, each student would work at his or her own narrative retellings by means of journals. For the students and for me, the entire experience was revealing, in the strict sense of the word.

At the end of the semester, I read sixty forty-page typed journals in which smart students reflected theologically about their own life stories. The effect on me was dramatic. First, I was changed by what I read: this was the moment when, for example, my lingering homophobia disappeared, as I learned of the struggles of my students to remain true to the way God had created them. Second, I became convinced of the singular power of narrative as a vehicle for revelation.

## Teaching and Writing/Writing as Teaching

On the basis of what I was learning with and from students — and in the light of my own less than completely satisfactory history with historical criticism, I began to work at what has continued to be my unsystematic constructive theological project, which I term "Ecclesial Hermeneutics." My last semester at Yale, I wrote *Decision Making in the Church: A Biblical Model.*[2] It went out of print with amazing rapidity and reappeared only in 1996 in an expanded version as *Scripture and Discernment: Decision Making in the Church.*[3] The book is about the church's decision making as a theological process

2. L. T. Johnson, *Decision Making in the Church: A Biblical Model.*
3. L. T. Johnson, *Scripture and Discernment: Decision Making in the Church.*

involving the experience of the Living God, the narration of such experience, the discernment of such experience, and the rereading of Scripture in light of what God is doing in the world. All this through an engagement with the long narrative in Acts 10–15 concerning the conversion of the Gentiles, in which all these elements are displayed.

My idea was that this sort of reading of Scripture could help create communities of readers who could learn the practice of discernment in local churches. It struck me as exceedingly odd that the compositions of the New Testament were all written for communities, yet in the entire history of biblical interpretation — apart from the practice of some groups like the Mennonites — the individual reader was always the subject of hermeneutical theory. How could the church as church read for church, that is, how could communities engage in the act of reading and read as though the ancient writings were actually addressed to them as a group?

Another question was how communities could read the New Testament as Scripture if the only mode of approach was through the classic historical-critical model. In an effort to provide an introduction/interpretation of the New Testament as the church's book, I began to draft *The Writings of the New Testament: an Interpretation.* I wrote it for a general readership, aware that it would also find service as a textbook. I invited readers to consider four dimensions of the New Testament: anthropological (its writers were struggling to interpret experience within their symbolic world), historical (that world was different from ours), literary (compositions were canonized and need to be read as compositions rather than as historical sources), and religious (the experiences being interpreted had to do with life before God in light of a crucified and raised Messiah). The anthropological and religious dimensions bring the ancient texts close to contemporary readers; the historical and literary dimensions require of contemporary readers an engagement with contexts other than their own.

These four dimensions fit within a model that provides an alternative to the historical-critical that I call "experience/interpretation," which is deeply influenced by the work of Luckmann and Berger on the social construction of reality.[4] The compositions of the New Testament are read, not as sources for a historical development, in light of which they are then interpreted, but as literary compositions arising out of and addressed to communities struggling to find meaning and coherent moral behavior in light of the crisis of meaning caused by their religious experience. It was my hope that students introduced to the New Testament in this manner would find themselves able to engage it dialogically, aware of their own social, cultural, and religious context, even as they conversed with compositions arising out of contexts different from theirs.[5]

This second writing project was clearly shaped by my teaching experience in a school of theology, but it was completed when I was a member of the department of religious studies at Indiana University in Bloomington (IU). Although I felt that my natural milieu was the seminary, this was the position I was able to get, and I was happy to return in 1982 to the place where I had received an M.A. in 1970. Now I was teaching New Testament introduction to undergraduates. But I found that the model I was developing was quite adaptable to students engaged in the study of humanities, and continued the same approach. I discovered that the way I taught exegesis (shorter papers, more frequent papers, interpretation rather than research) yielded the same positive results.

In fact, with bright undergraduates, I found that I was even more often stunned by student insight into the texts. But it was only toward the end of my ten years at IU that I came to the realization that that was the final stage of awareness before teaching the way I now do. The simple realization was that I had liberated and empowered bright readers, but *I was the only one benefiting from their insights!* Each semester I read over two hundred five-page interpretive papers. Among all the inevitable C- and B-efforts, there were always ten or fifteen papers of stunning excellence. I became even more convinced that investment in student brains was rewarded, and grew to understand how teachers stay intellectually alive because of being pushed by bright students. But I also came to see — just about the same

---

4. P. Berger and T. Luckmann, *The Social Construction of Reality: Treatise in the Sociology of Knowledge*; P. Berger, *The Sacred Canopy: Elements of a Sociological Theory of Religion*.
5. See Johnson, *The Real Jesus*, 167–77.

time I realized that the point of teaching was not my performance but theirs — that these bright students missed the same opportunity to learn from each other. Their best efforts in these large lecture classes were in the form of papers that were read only by me. The students were empowered, but they could not empower each other. This realization, however, could find expression only when I returned to a school of theology that made available to me the assistance of teaching associates.

In 1987, still at IU, I wrote *Faith's Freedom: A Classic Spirituality for Contemporary Christians.*[6] This was an attempt to fill in the missing element in my ecclesial hermeneutics, namely, the task of "reading human life" as a narrative of God's activity. If the capacities for this practice were not cultivated, then talk of a practice of discernment would be empty. The book built directly on my teaching experiences with small groups at Yale Divinity School, where we had worked at "Christian Existence as Life in the Spirit." It enabled me to distill some of the things I had learned about the specific aspects of life we had dealt with together: prayer, the use of possessions, sexuality, anger, power, freedom. But it also gave me the chance to write more fully about how I understood the basic elements of the human story as a drama of idolatry and grace, sin and faith. I find it interesting also that for the first time, this book also took account of my specific context in order to locate my work not as a statement of universal truth but as the partial witness of a middle-aged, white, male of the Midwest. Shortly after this book was published, I was called to teach at Candler School of Theology at Emory University. Now I had the chance, at last, to teach New Testament exegesis as an ecclesial practice.

## Preparing the Curricular Framework

Some heavy lifting was required before I could begin to teach exegesis as an ecclesial practice. The first task was curricular reform, which involved convincing my colleagues in Area I that New Testament Interpretation (*not* "Introduction") should command our best efforts

---

6. L. T. Johnson, *Faith's Freedom: A Classic Spirituality for Contemporary Christians.*

as the place to teach exegesis in a professional context, and that this could only be done as a required, two-semester course. When I arrived at Candler, quite a different attitude reigned. The twelve required hours in biblical study required of M.Div. students could be fulfilled without taking a survey of Hebrew Bible or New Testament at all. These courses were one-semester in length and were simply electives among others.

It was theoretically possible for a Candler student to graduate with an exposure to the Bible that consisted in the exegesis of Leviticus, Psalms, Luke, and Romans. Such "exegesis courses" had their merit, to be sure: students had intensive work in a single composition. But the model of exegesis was the same that had obtained in my description of Yale, ca. 1973, with a single major paper being produced at the end of the semester. More important, students were not required to have significant knowledge of the entire canonical collection, much less the process by which the writings were composed or put into the collection. The fundamental critical issues facing contemporary interpretation could therefore be bypassed, if the selection of exegesis courses was sufficiently cunning. The situation was analogous to medical students learning surgery for four parts of the human body, without first having had either gross anatomy or physiology.

It took some time for the Candler biblical faculty to work out and agree to a curricular structure for Area I. We finally committed ourselves to a four-semester sequence of Interpretation, with Hebrew Bible in the first year, and New Testament in the second year. We were aware that this would impact our elective offerings, but we decided that the gains in responsible coverage were worth the cost in smaller, more intensive courses. Because of the disparate amount of material in the two testaments, it was also agreed that Hebrew Bible would have less exegesis and more lecture/discussion format, and that New Testament would have one semester dedicated to the standard lecture format, followed by a semester of intensive practice in exegesis (involving, ideally, both testaments). As one might expect among academics, that broad framework of agreement has led to quite different ways of actually carrying out the task, depending on who is teaching the course. What follows is my way of doing New Testament Interpretation at Candler.

## *A Semester of Preparation*

The first semester of the course retains its character as a large lecture class in which mine is the dominant voice. Indeed, my voice is the more dominant since the students read my book as well as hear me lecture. I am content with this, for the point of the first semester is for them to learn the contents and concepts of the New Testament, and there is no better instrument for communicating both large amounts of material and a compelling vision of how that material fits together than a well-constructed series of lectures. The second semester, as I will show, is spent freeing them from my voice. A key to the success of the first semester, however, is that the students are required to read the entire New Testament through before I begin lecturing on any compositions. This requirement has two goals: the first is that they experience the New Testament as a living organism before it is subject to analysis; the second is that while they are reading, I am exposing the model and the materials that go into it, so that, subliminally, students are already beginning to think about the compositions they are reading from a different perspective.

The lectures begin with a self-conscious examination of the model used for the course, in comparison with other possible models. This enables students to understand that an interpretive standpoint is not simply a given, but can be chosen, and that different models (such as the historical-critical one) can yield different results. As stated above, the model has three moments dialectically related to each other: the construction of symbolic worlds, religious experience, and the re-interpretation of symbolic worlds in light of experience. The lectures begin with the symbolic world in which Christianity came into being, then move to the experiential claims of the first Christians and the problems those claims generated for understanding and for behavior, and then consider the various New Testament compositions, not in chronological sequence, but as examples of reinterpretation of the symbolic world within diverse manifestations of early Christianity: Synoptic, Pauline, Johannine, and others. The semester ends with a formal consideration of the New Testament as the church's book, with specific attention to the process and implications of canonization, and to a model for continuing interpretation within the life of faith.

Having the book to play off leaves me freer in each class session to approach specific issues in more detail, or from a fresh angle, and enables me to move from a more formal lecture style to a more dialogical style, since I am not obsessed with covering the material (the book does that). The students are exposed in the book to a single author's interpretation of every aspect of the New Testament, rather than a compendium of scholarly opinions. Although each chapter concludes with extensive annotated bibliographies, there are no footnotes and no "scholarly debates" within the exposition itself. I seek to model the boldness and first-person responsibility required of creative interpretation.

The symbolic world/interpretation model enables students to appreciate the diverse contexts of the ancient world more fully, since they learn not only facts about Greco-Roman and Jewish culture, but also how Greeks and Jews sought to interpret their sacred texts in response to changing circumstances and experiences. The same is the case with the early Christian literature. Students learn how each composition is the residue of an interpretive process within a community in which symbolic world (especially that of Torah), the founding resurrection experience, and subsequent experiences (conflict, persecution) generate new literature. As a result, students learn to view the New Testament as arising from a process of interpretation, and as the exemplary authorization for subsequent generations of Christians to enter into the same process.

Because this first semester is essentially a large lecture class, the work of the teaching associates,[7] if I am fortunate enough to have them, is minimal and not really necessary. There are no papers to grade. The teaching associates observe and learn my approach, help construct the multiple-choice and essay exams (all exams are "open-Bible," so that the questions can be more probing), and help grade them. It is in the second semester that the teaching become important, in fact necessary, to the pedagogy, and I am fortunate that Emory's

---

7. Ph.D. students at Emory typically serve two semesters as a "teaching assistant" and one semester as a "teaching associate," wherein they have increased participation in shaping and leading the course. In the first semester of the NT sequence here discussed Ph.D. students are typically in the role of "teaching assistant" and in the second semester "teaching associate." For simplicity I henceforth use "teaching associate" to refer to Ph.D. student assistants and associates.

Graduate Division of Religion can provide me a steady supply of highly talented Ph.D. students in New Testament to provide the assistance needed during the semester devoted to "exegesis as an ecclesial practice."

## *Unfolding the Practice*

In the second semester, the structure of the class changes dramatically. We meet in plenary sessions only three or four times, to enable me to trace for the class as a whole some major topic (such as the history of interpretation) or to give class-wide feedback on their progress in writing. Most of the sessions, students meet in groups of nine or twelve (the triad is important) in small rooms. These groups are carefully selected to provide as much diversity in age, gender, ethnicity, and religious background as is possible. They meet together throughout the semester as "ecclesial gatherings," covenanted to each other on matters of attendance and responsibility. The groups belong to themselves. To reinforce this point, the teaching associates and I rotate through the groups, facilitating the process for a different group each session.

From the beginning, I state that our purpose is to learn exegesis as an ecclesial practice, and that the best way to do this is to learn to practice together as a church. The class, then, is to be a laboratory for a practice that they, as pastors, will carry into their own congregations. I remind the students, a majority of whom are Methodist, how appropriate it is for the church to gather itself around the reading of the word of God, and how much these groups resemble the discipleship groups that started the Methodist movement. I appeal to the self-interest of all the students by declaring that the first death in any congregation is the death of the pastor's mind, that the reason for this sad state of affairs is that the pastor is often the only strong reader in the congregation, and that the pastor's own spiritual and intellectual life is best served by cultivating reading practices among others that can feed the pastor's mind in the same way that the powerful insights of bright students have kept teachers' minds alive for centuries.

I also remind the students and the teaching associates that to work together as church demands a high level of collaboration and a disposition toward the "edification of the group" rather than the gratification of the individual. I stress the notion of an excellence that is collaborative rather than competitive. The work the teaching associates and I do provides a model for the students, since they can observe the level of collaboration among us as we rotate through their groups. They know that we meet an hour before each class and an hour after, that we not only pass to each other the files containing the rosters and latest graded work to be given back, but also that we have consulted on the process to be engaged each session. They know that we know and discuss them as groups and assess them not only in terms of their individual work but also as part of a group process.

Within the groups, several kinds of activities take place. Each session begins with a prayer led by one of the group members, an obvious starting point if one meets as church, but also an important way of placing the scholarly activity within the realm of the Holy Spirit's power to transform. Throughout the semester, a considerable amount of attention is given to the individual stories of group members. At first, this is a matter of the name-game, all the more important because the teaching associates and I take longer to learn them, but also, as I have learned, because if personal relations are not constantly stressed, students prefer to withdraw, even in a small-group setting, to a more anonymous mode of presence. As the semester progresses, the importance of the personal story becomes more obvious as a factor in interpretation. The more students learn about each other (from each other), the more they learn how interpretation can be shaped by social location and personal biography. Even in this small group as a "context" for reading the New Testament, they learn how internally complex and diverse any given context can be.

The process of making the group and its members explicit as readers is aided by the reading of several books over the course of the semester. From different angles, each deals with the subject of New Testament interpretation, and although they are of unequal impressiveness, they work together well. One sketches, in a simple and straightforward way, a process for reading within communities that in some ways resembles what we do in this course.[8] Another

---

8. F. C. Tiffany and S. H. Ringe, *Biblical Interpretation: A Roadmap*.

is a collection of essays discussing the various methods employed by scholars in the interpretation of the Bible.[9] A third discusses in some depth the cultural conditioning of biblical interpretation in European, Latin American, and African American contexts.[10] A fourth engages the important issues concerning the New Testament's authority, adding an explicit feminist perspective.[11] Students engage these readings by preparing three typed, paragraph-length questions for each session devoted to a book or part of a book. These questions ensure reading, serve as preparation for more active participation in the discussion, and are, between classes, responded to in writing by the facilitator of that session.

Several pedagogical values are embedded in this way of reading secondary literature. At the simplest level, it fills the time gaps between the writing of papers. But it also reinforces the process in which the students are engaged as they write papers. Specifically, they learn that the questions they pose concerning the text are legitimate questions being asked by others. They learn that scholarly questions inevitably are also "person in the pew" questions, so that having a serious engagement with the issues is also good pastoral preparation. The writing of questions not only prepares students for class participation; it is a form of establishing egalitarianism: all group process privileges extraverts, who think as they speak, and marginalizes introverts, who must process thought before speaking. When their questions receive written response, students know they have been heard even when they could not speak, and teaching associates learn that the best and most thoughtful students are not necessarily the "blurters," whom, as insecure group facilitators, we are tempted to treasure. Finally, students slowly begin to realize that the process of learning how to interrogate a book and construct a good question parallels the process of biblical exegesis itself. Over the course of the semester, the teaching associates and I can trace the same improvement in the construction

---

9. S. L. McKenzie and S. R. Haynes, eds., *To Each Its Own Meaning: An Introduction to Biblical Criticisms and Their Application.*
10. B. K. Blount, *Cultural Interpretation: Reorienting New Testament Criticism.*
11. S. M. Schneiders, *The Revelatory Text: Interpreting the New Testament as Sacred Scripture.*

of these questions (eventually more than thirty) and the composition of papers.

The focus of the group's work is cultivating the practice of exegesis, which means the writing, reading, and evaluating of interpretive papers. Students are assigned five or six five-page papers over the course of the semester. Students all write on the same passages from representative genres in the New Testament (one paper on a Synoptic Gospel, one on John, two on Paul, one on a General Epistle, and one on Revelation). The idea is to actively engage a composition that one learned about in the first semester and, in so doing, establish one's own interpretive voice with respect to that composition. Although I adhere to the basic principles I developed already at Yale, I have modified the applications of them. I still insist that students use their own voice in interpretation. But I now have the opportunity to work with them more closely in the "how" of interpreting.[12]

Each paper is preceded by one or two workshops devoted to the skills we want them to exercise and the tools appropriate to employ for each exercise. The first assignment, for example, illustrates the use of the *synopsis,* a tool that will be valuable for as long as they read the first three Gospels. The next two papers use the *concordance;* two are necessary, because the concordance is such a tricky tool to use properly. In the fourth paper, students engage a *scholarly article* (that they must locate through research), which deals with the same passage in Paul that they are interpreting; the workshop preceding this assignment works through an actual "scholarly conversation" in journals that illustrates the value and limits of such engagement. Only in the fifth paper do students engage a single *commentary,* which they are to treat just as they do a scholarly article: the commentary is examined for its social location, presuppositions, and the like, as well as for its "reading" of the specific passage. This exercise is most revealing: students find themselves liberated from the fantasy that scholars somehow are better readers than they and their peers are. I want them to see the "scholarly conversation" taking place in books as an extension of the scholarly conversation that takes place in their

---

12. As a supplement to the instruction provided by the teaching associates and me, students have available G. D. Fee, *New Testament Exegesis: A Handbook for Students and Pastors.*

groups. In the final paper, students are allowed to use any or all of the tools they have learned, or none of them, as they interpret a passage from Revelation.

It is not so much the writing of papers as the reading and grading of them that is different within this pedagogy. Students bring their papers to the group, divide into smaller groups of three, and then exchange papers. Student A hears her paper being read out loud by student B, while student C listens. Each reading takes approximately fifteen minutes. After five minutes of feedback from the two who have heard the paper for the first time, the process continues for the other two papers. Then the group of twelve meets as a whole to discuss with the facilitator (who has spent the previous time listening from triad to triad) two things: what they have learned about the passage they did not know before this shared reading, and what they have learned about the process of exegesis from each other. This process takes place for every paper throughout the semester.

The results are dramatic. First, students' writing improves measurably. They realize the difference between writing "up" to impress a teacher in academese and writing "out" to colleagues who have devoted the same amount of time to the same passage. Oral delivery is wonderfully revealing of good and bad writing. Students start writing better. Second, students learn at once that, while there may be "bad" readings of a passage, there is no such thing as a single "right" reading. By hearing the work of intelligent and hard-working peers, they understand that a passage is open to many good and strong readings. They learn to think in terms of "responsible" exegesis: interpretation that is responsible both to the text being interpreted and to the community of interpretation. They also quickly understand the pertinence of inquiring into the context of a given interpreter, for if they all have read and worked on the same passage, the truly interesting question becomes how certain interpretations arose, why each reader saw what she saw or argued for the thesis that he did. Finally, by moving from the (very difficult) experience of work in the triads to the debriefing in their "ecclesial group," each participant gains a sense of being part of a larger effort in which the point is not how well they did but how well the group is doing.

The papers are read and graded by the teaching associates, and then read and graded a second time by me, and are returned to the students with extensive comments and corrections both from the teaching associate and from me within a week of handing them in. This is, to be sure, a grueling pace, but it makes the point that we are as serious about this as they are, or, to turn it another way, they need to be as serious about it as we are. They also see the work of collaboration in the way both the teaching associates and professor comments are side by side (I often underscore or comment on a teaching associate's comment), and in the way the professor assigns the final grade on the basis of a truly independent reading. This sort of attention also leads to real improvement in writing and interpretation skills.

As with the responses to the questions that are written in response to secondary literature, the process of reading and grading by the teaching staff assures students of individual attention. They are not swallowed by the group process and are therefore liberated to participate in it wholeheartedly. I have been asked why I don't have students collaborate on a paper, or do a "group exegesis." There are two reasons I stick with the format of individuals writing papers, even though the process of reading and evaluation is much more communal than in the normal New Testament class. The first reason is that we are educating leaders in the assembly, whose interpretive skills should be at a professional level and will be put to professional use in preaching and teaching. The capacity to see clearly, to know what they see, and to communicate what they see in convincing fashion demands the sort of responsible and individual development of skills that only repeated and carefully corrected papers can accomplish. The second reason is that it reinforces the point that every reader, even in the context of the church, needs to develop as a responsible reader. The group process works best when people come to it with something to offer as well as the willingness to receive. In fact, the process of writing and reading we use helps students understand the ecclesial importance of speaking in their own voice. At first, when they read about diverse social locations and underrepresented voices, students are tempted to think that they should somehow get these voices into their paper, not understanding that this is a form of alienation. The reading of papers in a group helps them see how important it is for them to speak from their own location, for it is in the social process that their own voice interacts with those of others who approach the text from another perspective.

A course that runs in this fashion demands a lot of the teaching staff. I have been blessed with gifted doctoral students who have entered into the spirit of the project with great enthusiasm and enviable pedagogical skill. Their willingness to meet for an hour before and after each class, to have their grading graded by me, to have their comments subject to my comments, to meet the expected pace of correcting and grading papers, suggests that they see in all of this a distinctive opportunity to learn something about teaching that a more laissez-faire model might not offer. I think they understand that they are truly receiving mentoring in pedagogy, even though spending an hour discussing why they gave a B+ to a student while I think it should be a B can be wearing. It is my sense that they, like me, are buoyed by the obvious progress being made by students and by the way a commitment to the brains and good will of students is repaid many times over by the quality of work they begin to do.

## A Practice in Process

I think that the course has done some things well. Students who work hard in it end up as more confident and more responsible interpreters of the New Testament, and as better writers. They have a good sense of the importance of context both at the time of the New Testament's writing and in the present. They learn to work collaboratively at a level of impressive excellence, pulling each other upward. They even, many of them, begin to have a practice of interpretation both for themselves and for the communities in which they will serve. All of them understand that it is possible to have a biblical scholarship that is of, for, and by the church.

The course also falls short of really teaching an "ecclesial practice" in a number of ways. A semester is not a long enough period of time. Six papers are still too few. The class working group is not really "church" because it shares only the three hours a week together. We cannot bring into the mix the personal narratives of faith in the way that would be appropriate in a congregation. The gap between the social reality of the academy and the church is perhaps most obvious in the need to write papers and have them graded. I have justified this above, but I am aware that within the life of an actual congregation, a more robustly oral form of participation is rightly the norm, and that the work students do in my class does not prepare them directly for the work of facilitation that they would need to do in the parish setting. But, as a "laboratory," perhaps at least we provide a sense of how they might make it work. When I have taken this class "on the road" with selected teaching associates and used the process in a completely oral fashion with church leaders and laity, it seems to work well.

There are notable costs in energy and enthusiasm demanded to teach this course well. Yet I am convinced that this way of doing things is worth that cost because of the transforming effect it has on students.

Chapter 11

# Twenty-Five Years of Contextualizing
## A RETROSPECTIVE FOR THE FUTURE
*Mary Elizabeth Mullino Moore*

The year was 1981, and I had just designed a new course, Ministry in Global Context, which was to be the anchor course for our new Master of Divinity curriculum at Claremont School of Theology (California). I was bursting with enthusiasm on the first day, so I began by explaining what I thought (and still think) was an exciting concept. Our class would explore three kinds of contextual consciousness: community consciousness, cultural consciousness, and global consciousness. We moved quickly then to introductions. First, I asked the group to name themselves and describe one formative community in their lives. These initial introductions went well; however, the next round was more complicated. The question was to name yourself in relation to one culture in which you have been formed. This question was energizing for the Asian, Asian American, Hispanic, and African American students, but challenging for the European Americans, who had difficulty identifying a culture. Some said: "I have never thought of being related to a culture," or, "Are you asking about my ancestry?" or, "What do you mean by culture?" Two European Americans had grown up in international settings, and they felt more connected to a global culture than to a particular culture in the United States. Already we were discovering some of the challenges of thinking contextually.

The purpose of this chapter is to draw insights, issues, and visions from my twenty-five years of effort in contextualizing theological education. Indeed, the course with which I began was part of a comprehensive effort in Claremont to contextualize theological education, as have been the last two decades of effort at Candler School of Theology. At Candler, the faculty has sought to ground theological education in first-year community-based courses, first identified as supervised ministry (SM) and later as contextual education. In these courses, all first-year master of divinity students serve in a clinical or social-service site, where they engage in action reflection and develop skills and insights as they reflect on themselves, ministerial action, diverse social contexts, and theology. This is followed in the second year with contextual education in ecclesial placements. In both Claremont and Candler, the particular purposes and configurations have varied markedly over the years, responding as one would expect to changing contexts. I will offer a few examples in this chapter — glimpses into the textures of contextual education in different times and places.

My intention is to analyze experiences from two schools, drawing upon representative moments in contextual education and seeking insights for the future. The analyses are limited by the restraints of retrospective and autobiographical analysis, but will hopefully be enriched by the engaged reflection of one who was intimately involved, further enriched by student responses and by reflection on larger theological movements that flowed under and around the contextual education efforts. Drawing from the case analyses, I will identify insights that emerge from the cases, concluding with proposals for more full-bodied contextual education in the future.

## Case Studies in Contextual Education

For me personally, the Ministry in Global Context course (with which I began) was foundational. Together with the educational theory that I love to study, it evoked new images of theological curriculum and teaching. Thus, the course was followed by several others in my personal history of theological education, all engaging students in contextual analysis, action reflection, and eco-social-theological reflection. In fact, one experimental course had preceded Global Context, plowing the ground for what was to come. In this chapter, I analyze some of these courses as miniature case studies, or snapshots of contextual education, describing the Global Context course in more detail, followed by a set of courses in Claremont, and a second set in Candler. Together these represent a span of time and geography, and a span also of subject matter and purpose.

## Ministry in Global Context

The purpose of Ministry in Global Context was to engage students in reflecting on their lives within local, communal, and global contexts. The purpose was further to prepare students for deeper analysis of global issues — the complex roots of these issues; the interplay among diverse peoples and contexts in creating and responding to these issues; the interweaving of theological, social, and environmental influences; and the possibilities for authentic ministry in such complex contexts. This was an exciting time to be considering such matters. It was an era when growing attention was given to issues of world hunger, poverty, and war, and when the mantra "think globally, act locally" was taking root in common parlance.

Of course, Claremont itself was in a particular context. Within the United States, Claremont had the most diverse student body of theological schools west of the Mississippi River, and it was also the most diverse of the thirteen United Methodist theological schools. Further, the 1980s was an era when the Association of Theological Schools was beginning its emphasis on globalization, sponsoring consultations on the urgency, possibilities, and dangers of globalizing theological education. Within such generative contexts, the Claremont faculty had decided to create the Global Context course to ground students' theological education.

The course began with the layers of analysis described above, and students wrote a paper on each layer: communal, cultural, and global consciousness. Readings included books and articles written about ministry in diverse contexts and about global issues and their local manifestations. Some of these issues were environmental; others focused on hunger, poverty, and structural injustice. Films were also helpful in amplifying and intensifying the issues, often leading to lively conversations with diverse perspectives. In addition, students wrote a large paper on one particular global-local issue in relation to practices of ministry, generating significant work on such topics as global hunger in relation to local food banks and global warming in relation to environmental practices of local congregations.

Perhaps the most interesting outcome of this course was the radical change that it underwent in the coming year. The course was well evaluated by students, and the dialogue and writing within the course were probing and insightful. My job, however, was simply to create the course, which a colleague would teach thereafter and would develop in ways that he chose. My interest in contextual education was the spur for the dean's inviting me to develop the original design. My teaching colleague was intrigued by the design, but he chose to reshape it radically, beginning the next year and continuing for a few years thereafter. He developed the course as a more issue-focused and lecture-intense class, attending particularly to environmental issues and to food and land. His course was consistently popular with students, who were drawn to my colleague's passionate concern about issues that also concerned them. In reflecting back on his pedagogical shift, I think that it too was a reflection of the context. We were in an era in which urgent issues captured people's imaginations, and in which the details of contextual analysis seemed somewhat esoteric. Though students gave high evaluations to the course that I taught, my colleague's shift was also well received by the next generations.

What did I learn from this early experiment in contextual education? *First, I learned how energizing and illuminating contextualizing can be.* In the Global Context course, we learned a great deal about global issues, and we probed those issues in our own personal, communal, and cultural lives. In the process, *we discovered the complexity of contextual analysis.* Analyzing contexts is counter-intuitive for people who have been schooled to think of themselves as mostly autonomous individuals (with community and culture as a backdrop) or to think of themselves as generic, as is often the case for European Americans. This was one of the challenges and rich discoveries of the class. *Further, I discovered that contextual education can be done in many different ways.* Though I thought I had designed a strong course that could be developed in ever-richer ways over ensuing years, I recognized that my colleague, who continued and changed the course, also had important and effective ways of teaching contextually. We were part of a large enterprise with many different goals and pathways, or "curricula" in educational terms. *Finally, I learned that one contextual experiment leads to others.* Such teaching is sufficiently engaging and challenging that I was "caught" by the contextual virus and have continued to teach contextually ever since. Similarly, such teaching spreads in a faculty, so that experiments by one or two people sometimes lead to experiments by others. *On a more sober note, I learned that contextual teaching can easily lapse into occasional mentions of contextual realities, generalized discussion of issues, or educational experiments that are left to a few faculty whose fields or personal preferences lend themselves to such teaching.*

## Two Claremont Experiments with Engaged Pedagogy

The years surrounding the Global Context course involved further experiments, this time with more attention to engaged pedagogy. Two courses in particular contributed to the growing contextual emphasis in Claremont's curriculum. Both sought to involve people in action reflection that could uncover realities of the world, sources of Christian life and ministry, and religious practices informed by those realities and sources. The curricular reflection that the Claremont faculty had done for several years not only inspired such courses, but it also cleared a path for us to develop them.

**Curriculum for a Non-Expansive World.** Shortly before the Global Context course was envisioned, Allen Moore and I had developed a summer-intensive course called Curriculum for a Non-Expansive World. This was during the same period (also 1981) when concern about global hunger and poverty was strong in the churches. Students and church leaders frequently bemoaned disparities between what they read in newspapers and learned in theological classrooms and churches. Further, they regretted the failure of church curriculum resources to help them address these disparities. Seeking to respond to these concerns, Allen and I worked with a team of faculty colleagues, church leaders, and students to create a collaborative learning experience for students, church professionals, and faculty. Both the teaching team and students were diverse in ethnicity and life experience, creating a rich mix of gifts and perspectives. Our intent was to engage

people in exploring issues of economic disparity, global connectedness, environmental destruction, and Christian response. The syllabus
expressed this purpose:

> This course is designed as an intensive educational experience in
> which we face issues of a non-expansive world and related edu-
> cational issues. We will explore theoretical and practical issues,
> experiment with alternative ways of Christian teaching, engage
> in field experiences, and do constructive curriculum-building.[1]

Because this course preceded the publication explosion on global
consciousness, we created a book of readings that drew from diverse
sources, including essays, newspaper clippings, curriculum samples,
and working documents that we had created. Film was a major component of the class, and we viewed several films and film clips in
relation to particular topics. We also read books on biblical interpretation in relation to current economic realities, ministry with the
lectionary, home-grown curriculum, and innovative education. Much
of the class focused on integrating the multiple sources of knowledge into a coherent whole and designing curriculum resources that
were responsive to global issues and local communities. To that end,
we accented central themes through the eight-day period, and we
approached them through multiple sources and activities.

In relation to food and its role in sustenance and justice, we studied world hunger, the role of food in diverse cultures, and monastic
practices of shared eating. We read and heard introductions to these
traditions, and we engaged with them, having a Korean meal prepared and introduced by Korean students, a Thai meal prepared by
the local Thai community, a Benedictine silent meal with readings
as we ate, and so forth. The people who provided these meals and
explanations were not only paid a stipend, but many of them also participated in the course, thus engaging in the pre- and post-reflections
with the community.

Another theme was Sabbath, for which we studied biblical texts
and writings about Sabbath, focusing on Sabbath practices in relation to theological, ecological, and human rationale. Each participant

---

1. Syllabus, Curriculum for a Non-Expansive World, 1981.

spent time in the first few days planning her or his Sabbath celebration (for the Sunday at the center of the class). We encouraged one another to plan a Sabbath that would respond to the deepest intentions of Jewish and Christian traditions and would challenge us and our relations (families, congregations, and friends) toward simpler and more faithful living. On the following Monday, we reflected upon our Sabbath experiences and how those experiences related to traditional practices and understandings, to practices of diverse Christian communities, and to our hopes for more enduring changes in our personal and communal lives. Allen and I had planned Sabbath with our children, for example, deciding not to use a car on Sunday to spend our full day after church in family activities. We walked to and from church, we had a leisurely and simple lunch at home, and we spent the afternoon walking in the botanical gardens. As a side note, our children did not like this Sabbath idea, and they balked as we did it. Unlike children who grow up in strict Sabbath-observing communities, they recognized this as a strange experiment. They were also intrigued, however, helping us to plan the day as well as to live it. We were able to continue in some of what we began on that weekend, but the more difficult parts (e.g., not using the car) fell away quickly. Several years later, our daughter recalled that weekend as a great time (much to her parents' surprise).

This course had values beyond the immediate. *Personal transformation was potent,* evoking testimonies many years later. *Further, participants created curriculum designs and resources that they and others used in their communities* over the coming months. The results were stunning, and we received reports throughout the following year of how these ideas and resources had taken root in the diverse communities represented. As one might surmise, *this course was a labor- and time-intensive moment of teaching, which was fruitful beyond our imagination.* Unfortunately, we never repeated it, turning instead to other responsibilities and requirements within our regular theological curriculum. On the other hand, this course had lasting effects on participants, including Allen and me. For my part, I developed other courses informed by this early one. In Education and Story, for example, I engaged students with narrative theology and pedagogy, and students produced video stories for use in churches and other venues. In Sacred Teaching, we produced a book of resources for use in diverse settings.

**Communal Learning and Care of the Earth.** A second innovation in theological teaching became a more enduring part of the Claremont curriculum when Frank Rogers and I created a course called Communal Learning and Care of the Earth — a course that we repeated together and separately from 1991 to 1999, with enduring influences on our other teaching to the present day. Communal Learning moved me, as a contextual teacher, toward a more direct focus on analyzing and acting within the immediate seminary community, seeing the school as both home and laboratory for engaged learning. It also moved me toward teaching in a rhythmic way — developing rhythms of ritual, study, shared eating, and work. These rhythms reflect monastic traditions of formation and daily life, and they also form a learning community that reveres, learns, acts, and celebrates together.

Communal Learning was aimed toward engaging students with the earth in relation to movements of the Spirit. We involved students in analyzing different parts of the Claremont campus, sending groups out on the second day of class to explore the campus and discern places of joy and pain. In successive weeks, we continued this analysis, drawing upon educational, theological, and ecological resources to complexify and deepen our thinking. Simultaneously, we asked students to develop projects for these campus sites. The first class began a meditation garden, stirred originally by a soggy area beside the chapel where people could not walk or sit and where trees were stunted by the poor drainage. In later semesters, students added their dreams and continued creating the garden. With a supportive dean and president, collaboration with many colleagues and students, and a trustee who dreamed of a biblical garden, the project grew into the "biblical-meditation garden." We planted indigenous and endangered plants, which were also plants named in the Bible. We created a pond. We created seating places. We added a mural to the retaining wall, which reads, "Let justice flow down like waters."

Other groups in the Communal Learning classes did other projects, including a campus vegetable garden, a recycling system, a campus program on water conservation, an Earth Care Fair, building audits, and so forth. These projects spread through the community, not only in terms of participation, but also in terms of institutional ownership. The recycling program, for example, became a regularized part of campus maintenance. Further, the original projects and their extensions led to grant-writing and the development of a master landscape plan for the school, including an outdoor amphitheater for classes and informal gatherings. Step by step, the plan took place over a period of years, continuing after I departed Claremont and after Frank redirected his energies toward drama ministries with youth.

What also continued was our approach to pedagogy. Not only was the class directed to projects of the students' making, but the class sessions were designed to promote reading, meditation, and reflection that would enlarge our visions and equip our work. The sessions themselves, longer than typical class sessions, were designed in the form of a Benedictine community, following regular rhythms: gathering ritual, study, shared eating, shared work, and closing ritual. Each session was designed around the theme and assignments for the day, and students took turns in preparing the gathering rituals and eating. Frank and I planned the study section, and we worked with the teams as they developed their shared work, providing guidance and helping with arrangements and supplies as needed.

As the Curriculum for a Non-Expansive World course, this class was time- and labor-intensive. Also like the Curriculum course, it generated energy within the class and in the larger community that enjoyed and joined the fruits of our labors. Eventually, the projects of the Communal Learning class led to campus work days and other projects that were led by the Eco-Justice Task Force, and some of the projects were continued by the Maintenance Department of the school. Indeed, we worried at one time that our projects were adding unduly to the work of the maintenance staff, but the staff worked with us to develop manageable systems and procedures. At times, we saved them work, as in the year we painted the children's playground. At other times, we added to their burdens, as in the garden expansions. They generously worked with us, however, to create a strong and equitable partnership.

Reflecting on these two Claremont courses and the engaged pedagogy of each, I learned much about contextual education. *Contextualizing contributes to full-bodied learning, integrating textual, communal, and action learning in a messy and generative whole.* It raises profound questions and insights, which continue to emerge long after the course ends. *It requires months of preparation and intensive work throughout the course.* For this reason, *contextual teaching is best done (at least initially) by teaching teams,* who contribute diverse visions and gifts. The ideal is a partnership of faculty, students, local communities, and institutions. These partnerships may emerge gradually, however, and be inspired and built by contextual teaching over time. *Finally, such teaching transforms people* — inspiring discovery, critical reflection, and action; evoking questions about our personal and communal lives; and contributing to the ethos and ethics of institutional life.

## Continuing Engaged Pedagogy in New Contexts

I was forever changed by the contextual courses in Claremont and the students who participated in them. Such teaching has continued to shape my teaching at Candler School of Theology, where I joined the faculty in 1999. I will reflect on the Candler courses more briefly, but will note especially the new discoveries that emerged with each course. The purpose here is not to detail all imaginable contextual courses, but to give a textured picture of such teaching as a source for reflecting on the future.

**Contextual Education I and II.** While the formal contours of Contextual Education I and II are described in the Introduction of this book, I will describe these experiences in the form of discoveries and rediscoveries about contextual teaching. My Contextual Education I experience has included teaching with students in three sites — a parish-sponsored homeless ministry, a learning-partner ministry with developmentally disabled adults, and a prison ministry. In my experience of Contextual Education II, students were serving local churches, a hospice site, and a residential facility for people living with emotional challenges. These experiences have led me to three primary discoveries, though I recognize how much more could be said.

*First, I discovered that meeting with a group of students for the prime purpose of contextual reflection every week builds strong relational bonds and strengthens students' ministries.* In Contextual Education I, this was magnified by the fact that the students were new to Candler, making adjustments of many kinds. They were also my advisees, and I was to meet with them throughout their Candler years. The first year bonds intensified the advisement relation, and the final semester interview was consistently powerful, with students referencing their first Contextual Education experience as well as the ways they had grown personally, academically, and professionally over the Candler years. The bonds were also strong with one another, and students who were very different became close friends, supporting and challenging one another well into their post-Candler futures.

*Second, I rediscovered that team teaching is vital in contextual education.* Being paired with site supervisors in Contextual Education I and with a pastor in Contextual Education II, I learned much from their wisdom. Further, we were able to share the load and offer diverse forms of mentoring with students. My relationship with each Contextual Education partner was different; it was even different in the two years that I partnered with the same person. This diversity kept us all fresh and contributed to our learning as well as that of students. I was grateful for such strong partners each year and grateful too that we were jointly able to be flexible in working styles. This said, the flexibility of partnering went beyond personal abilities. The commonly valued Contextual Education program, which faculty had devised over time and site supervisors had helped shape, created an ethos and opportunity that maximized our abilities to work together.

*Third, I discovered that contextual learning often takes place in crisis, interpreted both as opportunity and as traumatic event.* The crisis may be a new opportunity to preach or counsel in the prison or to preach in a congregation. It may also be the traumatic experience of seeing your learning partner neglected and mistreated by an unstable parent, or being fired by your local church, or being caught in a tangled conflict between a pastor and congregation. The Contextual Education setting in which faculty, supervisor, and wise peers reflect together on such situations is almost always therapeutic and insightful; it usually offers guidance as well. This is not always the case, of course, and contextual education also presents challenges for learning when the group process is less than adequate to the situation. Even in these situations, however, the ongoing relationships open possibilities for continued processing and learning.

**Prophetic Pioneers in Religious Education.** Another Candler course draws upon oral history methodology. In Prophetic Pioneers in Religious Education, the primary printed sources are biographies, autobiographies, and oral histories. In addition, we study the art of oral history, and students prepare and conduct oral history interviews within the class. In 2004, the class interviewed three pioneers, and we interviewed another two in 2006. These interviews have been sponsored by the Oral History Project and funded by the Wabash Center for Teaching and Learning in Theology and Religion. The connections with a larger project and the special funding have enabled us to do more extensive work than would have otherwise been possible.[2] This has also allowed students to contribute to a larger project that will be available to churches and local communities as well as to the Pitts Theology Library archives. To have the opportunity to make such a significant contribution without carrying the entire load of a multilayered, multi-year project is itself significant for contextual education.

The purpose of Prophetic Pioneers is to "explore religious education history, issues, and visions through life story, contextual analysis, and educational theories, practices, and cultural 'products.'"[3] To that end, the course involves students in studying life history accounts, exploring education in diverse settings, and conducting and analyzing interviews and writings of living historians. After the first round of this course, Claire Bischoff and I did an extensive analysis of it in relation to education for justice and peace, discovering

---

2. The Oral History Project is a seven-year project sponsored by Women in Theology and Ministry, Candler School of Theology, Emory University, Atlanta. Funding for 2003–7 has been provided by Wabash Center for Teaching and Learning in Theology and Religion. We have interviewed thirty-one women thus far, including women in diverse ministries and life circumstances. The particular women interviewed in the Prophetic Pioneers class are involved in some form of religious education.

3. Syllabus, Prophetic Pioneers in Religious Education, Fall 2004. The same purpose statement appears in the 2006 syllabus as well.

that such a class contributes significantly to respectful relationships and creative agency within and beyond the classroom.[4] In the context of the present chapter, the student responses will yield other discoveries. What students particularly appreciated in the class were the active learning process, the practicality of our work for future ministry, encounters with cultural and pedagogical diversity, engagement with prophetic pioneers, the experience of building a learning community and practicing hospitality with one another and the pioneers, and the opportunity to participate in oral histories and an experimental pedagogy. The biggest challenges for students were the shifts that took place as we moved through the course. For example, one pioneer was not able to join us and her group had to shift to another pioneer mid-course. Further, because we were developing this as an experimental course, we did not map out the weight of assignments until mid-semester, which frustrated one student in particular.

This course, as the others I have described, had much to teach. *First, it revealed that contextual teaching does not necessarily focus on contexts as the primary subject matter.* This course was thoroughly contextual, but not labeled as such. The major purpose was to study religious education history, theory, and practice *through* the intellectual tools of contextual and life history analysis. *Second, I learned the value of involving students in project learning that is part of a larger movement,* transcending the bounds of the class. In this class, students knew that the quality of their work was for a purpose that went beyond their own learning and performance; their work would contribute to others' learning in a tangible way. Being part of a larger movement had the additional advantage of involving students in a project that they did not have to invent. They could benefit from what had already been done and could participate in the middle of the project, using their creativity but not having to create the entire project from beginning to end. As director of the Oral History Project, I could do groundwork to set the stage for the students and

---

4. Claire Bischoff and Mary Elizabeth Mullino Moore, "Cultivating a Spirit for Justice and Peace: Teaching through Oral History," *Religious Education* (in press).

also leave them freedom to conduct interviews in ways that interested them, knowing that I could conclude the interview protocols at a later time. Finally, *we learned that contextual learning, especially when it involves team projects, can cultivate human understanding, compassion for people of diverse times and places, and vision for future action.*

**Global Feminisms and Christian Theology.** One final course is also thoroughly contextual, though the subject matter is feminist theologies. The contextual complexity of this class is implicit in its purpose statement:

> to *evoke* the theological passions of the class, to *explore* the passions and perspectives of women in different parts of the world and different periods of history, to *engage* theological questions with critical imagination, and to *construct* theological perspectives and actions for the sake of future, especially for the wellbeing of women in the church and world.[5]

This purpose statement reveals several contexts that are important to the class: the class members themselves who form the class's primary context; the women whom we study in texts and other media, women from diverse times and places; and future contexts in which students will exercise their vocations.

Contextual analysis is built into several aspects of the class, beginning with my own decision to focus a class on global feminisms, which immediately raises contextual questions. A second contextual element is our attention to students' immediate contexts, as in the first two short papers of the class. The first paper is to describe and reflect on a deep passion in your own life, and the second focuses on a struggle in your life or the life of a woman whom you know well. A third contextual element is built into the rubric for analyzing the texts. I ask students to address each text with several questions:

1. What are the author's deepest passions?

2. What does the author most want readers to understand? to question? Why?

---

5. Syllabus, Global Feminisms and Christian Tradition, Spring 2006.

3. What in the author's contexts, traditions, and religious experiences have impelled her to write this book or essay?

4. What is the unique contribution of this work?

Another contextual element is asking students to observe their contexts (e.g., to observe and analyze a worship service) and to create a series of context-relevant resources as part of their thematic work throughout the course. Students, together with an editorial team, later refine these creations into a book of resources, which we make available through Candler community networks. One final aspect of contextualizing in this course is the final paper, in which I ask students to construct a theological position on a selected theme or doctrine, constructing their positions in relation to theological traditions, contextual realities, and pressing issues in the world, especially for women.[6]

Like Prophetic Pioneers, this class uses the intellectual tools of contextual description and analysis to study another subject matter, namely, feminist theologies. Like Ministry in Global Context (the first class described in this chapter), Global Feminisms encourages community, cultural, and global consciousness. Like Curriculum for a Non-Expansive World, it involves resource development. Like Communal Learning and Care for the Earth, it involves rhythms in the learning process, plus description and analysis of the immediate contexts in which students function. I share these comparisons because they teach me something further about contextual learning. In addition to the insights derived from each particular course, *I discover that, cumulatively, contextual teaching and learning can inform teaching across disciplines.* Although disciplines are distinct from one another and contextual investigation may take different forms in different subject areas, contextual approaches also cross disciplines. *Further, contextual teaching in diverse subject areas illumines theological study in general.* It especially encourages interdisciplinary integration that is grounded in life situations. *Finally, contextual*

---

6. I ask students to address the central question: What perspectives and actions are most significant to retrieve, question, form, and re-form in relation to your theme, especially as you reflect on the theme in relation to women's lives?

*education equips people for significant wrestling between theological traditions and pressing realities of the contemporary church and world.*

## Contextual Directions for the Future

In the case reflections, I have already identified discoveries regarding contextual education, uncovering values and possibilities as well as dangers. The most obvious value is the transformative nature of contextual teaching. Persons, and sometimes institutions, undergo visible change in perspectives, values, and practices. Such changes often point to radical transformations in people's deepest values and guiding visions. The dangers are that people become awakened to enormous problems in the world, and the comfort of separating theological knowledge from these problems is forever disrupted.

During this past summer, I saw three former students who now live on three different continents. Our meetings were in diverse settings, but the stories resonated with one another. These three people described their present work and then, much to my surprise, thanked me for engaging them in active approaches to teaching and ministry. Two pointed explicitly to contextual elements of my teaching, citing, for example, my practice of bringing cases, videos, and materials from educational institutions in the Pacific Islands, Asia, and Africa, where new contextual educational forms are being developed. All three of these people are actively engaged with their current communities, continually seeking and creating ways to respond authentically and fruitfully. One is creating international dialogues between former colonizing and colonized peoples. One teaches public school teachers to work with students who live on the social margins because of poverty and other hard life experiences. One combines theological teaching with ministry in a multicultural, impoverished congregation. I do not take credit for these remarkable people and the work they are doing. The three unexpected meetings did, however, awaken me to connections between contextual teaching and vocational vision, fueling my passion to reflect in this chapter on future directions for contextual education.

## Developing Contextual Consciousness

One important direction for contextual education is to help people develop contextual consciousness. I first became aware of this need in working on the two courses of 1981. At this time, social-historical criticism had long been a prominent method in biblical and historical studies, but contextual analysis emerged more slowly in systematic and practical theologies, perhaps because both disciplines had long traditions of offering guidance for the church and for Christian thought and life. Contextual consciousness had a slow entry into many realms of theological thinking and even into theological education. When it first emerged, it was more focused on the skills of a pastor than on the complexities of societies, cultures, and communities in which churches existed, theologies were formed, and Christian practices were manifest. Even now, the multiple layers of communal, cultural, and global contexts are rarely investigated in relation to theology and one another. Several challenges lie ahead: equipping people (especially people in dominant cultures) to develop contextual consciousness; creating honest and respectful dialogues with diverse peoples; and equipping people with pastoral, analytic, and interpretive skills with which to face the overwhelming complexity of their worlds.

## Developing Engaged Pedagogies

A second insight is the importance of engaged pedagogies. Such pedagogies involve teachers and students in reflective actions that are important to them and to other communities, proceeding through an action-reflection process that yields wisdom, critique, and reformed action. Engaged pedagogies can take many forms. The most familiar forms in theological education are the action-reflection opportunities associated with internships and other ministerial placements. Other forms involve people in projects, such as the ecological, curricular, and oral history projects described in this chapter. Still other forms of engaged pedagogy involve shaping class sessions to engage people with the multiple dimensions of the subject under study, as we did in the rhythms of ritual, study, work, and eating in Curriculum for a Non-Expansive World and in Communal Learning and Care for the

Earth. In the cases of this chapter, we can also see engaged pedagogy in weekly assignments, such as assignments to observe a community or create a resource.

Engaged pedagogies often make contributions beyond the bounds of a particular course. Many contextual classes of this chapter, for example, created resources and new approaches for ministry, which were for use beyond the classroom. The Communal Learning class even led to radical institutional change in Claremont over a period of ten years. Engaged pedagogies involve people in significant work in dialogue with historical traditions, theoretical constructs, and social analysis, thus contributing fresh insight combined with more tangible outcomes.

## Developing Teaching Teams and Learning Communities

A third direction for contextual education is to develop teaching teams and learning communities. Almost all of my contextual courses have been team-taught, at least initially. Collaboration enhances contextual course design because contextualizing requires diverse teaching gifts, it involves heavy preparation that is best shared, and it is especially creative when a team works together to break old patterns. Teaching teams are even richer when they involve regular teaching faculty, church and community leaders, and others (including staff in such cases as the Communal Learning course). What is rarely done but is important to the future is to develop interdisciplinary teaching teams, enabling people with different disciplinary expertise to bring that expertise to bear on educational design and contextual reflection. Further, contextual education works especially well when students are also involved in collaborative learning, either working together on projects or building relationships as they reflect on their contextual experiences.

## Developing Multi-dimensional Contextual Offerings

A fourth direction is to develop a broad range of contextual offerings. One of my discoveries in twenty-five years of contextual teaching is that contextual courses can easily become the work of a few specialized teachers. This was especially true in Claremont, where contextual teaching was not required of all teaching faculty.

On the other hand, one of the challenges at Candler, where *all* faculty teach Contextual Education, is to insure that contextual education courses are indeed taught contextually. Having said this, I do not intend to suggest that there is only one way to teach contextually, for one of my early insights is that many ways are appropriate and effective. People will discover diverse ways to teach standard contextual courses (such as Contextual Education I and II), as well as diverse and wide-ranging subject matters and approaches for other contextual courses. I have personally been involved in contextual teaching in field courses, constructive theology, practical theology, and religious education. This experience is not comprehensive, but it is wide enough to raise my hopes about interdisciplinary teaching in other subject areas. Consider a biblical course, for example, in which students study texts as they also study communities' engagement with the Bible. The possibilities are limitless.

## Engaging in Generative Experiments

Another direction for the future is to encourage generative teaching experiments. Indeed, I have discovered that one generative experiment leads to another. One way to investigate and expand contextual teaching is to initiate experiments that are intended to be good courses in themselves, with the expectation that they will also inform future teaching. Even when the particular experiments are not repeated, they affect faculty's teaching and students' learning in further courses. Because contextual courses are usually time-consuming, they are often not repeated, at least with frequency. On the one hand, this is unfortunate. On the other hand, these experiments may lead to modest and larger changes in other courses, permeating them with contextual elements and purposes. Further, these experiments can contribute to larger movements in teaching, learning, and research, as in the Oral History Project.

## Responding Authentically to Human Communities and Crises

One other direction is suggested by the case studies of this chapter, namely, the need to encourage authentic responses to human communities and to human and ecological crises as they emerge. All teaching needs to be responsive to the people involved and the contexts in which they live.[7] Contextual education takes particular responsibility for such responsiveness, however. One advisee told me at the end of her Master of Divinity program that Contextual Education I was one of her favorite courses, though she was disappointed in many aspects of her theological education. This was a superb student, who had excelled in all of her work. Her response surprised me, so I asked her to explain. She said that Contextual Education was "real," engaging her with people who were facing real struggles and reflecting with others about what was happening in these situations.

Added to this response are less happy experiences with students who were frustrated (even angry) with some aspect of Contextual Education, either a crisis in the placement or some discomfort with the Contextual Education Seminar Group. I have experienced only a small number of these problems, but they have been difficult. Though every one of these students learned something significant in the process, the experiences themselves were intense. I have come to believe that contextual education inevitably evokes crises, small and large. Thus we need to be intentional. We need to create opportunities for people to engage in messy situations, build supportive and reflective communities, and teach skills through which difficult experiences can become opportunities for learning and positive transformation. If such learning opportunities are grounded in living communities, they cannot produce guaranteed outcomes, but the opportunities will be abundant.

## Contextual Practices for the Future

In light of the future directions to which I have pointed, theological educators also need to reflect on practices for contextual learning. The cases in this chapter illumine such practices, and the insights have been sharpened for me by a recent paradigmatic experience. As I was writing this chapter, a good friend was living her last weeks with cancer. I spent a portion of every day in the hospital, sometimes sitting with her quietly and sometimes joining in lively chatter with my friend and her family and friends. I could never know when I

---

7. C. A. Bowers and Flinders, *Responsive Teaching*.

approached my friend's room how she was that day, nor how her family was doing. On some days, I stayed a few minutes, recognizing a need for her family to be alone. On other days, I sat with my friend a few hours so her family could go home and rest. Sometimes the family told me what they needed; on other days, I had to discern their needs from small signs. Further, this much-loved woman had many friends, so I also had to make judgments about when to be present and when to step out so other friends could have private time. These many judgments helped me discern when to visit and when to stay away, when to enter my friend's room and when to stay in the waiting room, when to speak, when to listen, and when to sit quietly and pray.

This poignant period in my friend's life reveals much about the skills of contextual education. My friend's context was not only her bedside, but also the waiting room and the busy wing where nurses and doctors did their healing and caring work. The context also included hospital hallways, where I passed hospital personnel (tired, excited, worried, burdened, or busy); hospital in-patients and out-patients (dealing with diverse forms of illness and preventative care); and family and friends of patients who faced varying degrees of good and bad news about their loved ones. As I walked the hallways, I needed to read the signs of those whom I passed. I needed to adjust my greeting and demeanor to what I saw on their faces. The context also included health care plans, hospital structures and ethos, hospice institutions, and the human diversity of patients, families, and care-givers. This story is a microcosm of contextual education, revealing some of the contextual practices needed to respond to a whirlwind of complexity.

**Revering.** One practice is to revere the people with whom we engage in contextual education, and also to revere the land, water, and air of the context.[8] Reflecting on the hospital context of my friend, I was aware that my visits were better attuned if I walked the hospital hallways and entered my friend's room with respect for what people were doing and what they were facing in this place of healing

---

8. I have written about this teaching practice in Moore, *Teaching from the Heart: Theology and Educational Method.*

and dying. In teaching contextual courses, I have learned again and again that revering the earth (as in Communal Learning), revering the people of a learning community, and revering the peoples with whom a class engages are critical if we are to build respectful relations and to learn well. Revering is also important if a class is to make a real contribution to the community or setting with which it is engaged.

**Reading signs.** Another practice is to read the signs that are available in a particular setting. In the hospital, the signs are faces, movements, words, and sometimes posted signs. In other settings, the same kinds of signs are present, in addition to architecture and landscape, visual symbols, music and the arts, community actions, community stories, printed documents, historical artifacts, and so forth.

**Analyzing and interpreting.** The practice of analyzing and interpreting is also critical if we are to understand what is going on in a situation, to learn from the context, and to make judgments regarding our responses. This is an ongoing process of discovery. In the hospital setting, I continually analyzed what I saw and heard, interpreted the meaning, analyzed further, and changed my interpretations. The process had no end.

The same process takes place in contextual teaching, but the analysis and interpretation may be focused on a large community, institution, or social context. When my Contextual Education I group was engaged in ministries in Metro State Prison for Women, for example, the site supervisor (with support from me) did an excellent job of introducing the site during the first month, beginning with handouts and the prison website, followed by a visit and many stories and words of wisdom. On final evaluation forms, however, students wrote that they had needed a better introduction to the prison. I have continued to ponder these responses. Of course, our teaching team could have done some things better. In retrospect, however, I think that what we needed most to do was to explain in advance that the group could *not* know the prison well in the beginning, but would move to ever deeper understanding during the year. In reality, no one can introduce a context adequately because "knowing" a context requires analysis and interpretation over time. That is what did happen in the prison. By the end of the year, students were engaged in sophisticated analysis and insightful interpretation about the prison itself, the people who lived and worked there, and the prison system in Georgia and the United States.

**Changing responses to changing situations.** Another critical practice is to change responses to changing situations. In the hospital, I never knew how my friend and her family would be when I arrived. One day they were laughing and talking vigorously. On other days, they were moving slowly and sadly, crying, or sleeping. My role was to be present with them in the particular context of a particular day. This is the ongoing role of contextual education as well. Certainly our students who spent four hours in prison ministry each week discovered a constantly changing context. The inmates moved to other prisons or were released or were disappointed to discover that they would not be released after all. An inmate who was eager to talk one week avoided the chaplain intern the next week and then wanted more conversation in the week after that. In the Communal Learning class, we discovered constant change as well. The institutional receptivity, needs, and collaboration changed over time, even in the course of a single semester. In the Prophetic Pioneers class, the changes were often related to the living pioneers whom we were interviewing. Both the teaching team and the students made adjustments throughout the semester and learned a lot about flexibility in the process. Such change is part of any context and, thus, is part of contextual teaching in its many forms.

**Responding to crisis.** This discussion leads naturally to the practice of responding to crises. If teachers and learners are engaged in the practices described thus far, they will usually be alert to crises as they arise. In the hospital setting, I was aware of changes in my friend's health or in her family's spirits, and usually aware of crises or turning points. In contextual education, such crises emerge in many forms. In the course on Curriculum for a Non-Expansive world, a crisis emerged during a festival occasion with a Thai meal. None of us ate the head and tail of the fish that we were served, and the Thai people were insulted that we would be so unappreciative and wasteful. This led to important conversations about Thai culture and about food practices in a "non-expansive world." In Contextual Education

I and II, crises often emerge in the ministry settings, and they can be quite dramatic, as when a student was caught unwittingly in a conflict between a pastor and congregation. Our challenge in contextual education is to develop skills to discern, analyze, interpret, and respond appropriately to crises when they emerge. This is an important aspect of contextual learning, which needs to be expected and embraced.

The directions and practices that I have named in this chapter are not comprehensive. Much more could be said. What is important, however, is to continue the dialogue so that contextual education can permeate theological curricula more fully and bear abundant fruit.

# Bibliography

Allen, Ronald J., and John C. Holbert. *Holy Root, Holy Branches: Christian Preaching from the Old Testament.* Nashville: Abingdon, 1995.

Alter, Robert. *The Art of Biblical Poetry.* New York: Basic Books, 1985.

Anderson, Gerald H. *Biographical Dictionary of Christian Missions.* New York: Macmillan Reference USA, 1997.

Berger, Peter L. *The Sacred Canopy: Elements of a Sociological Theory of Religion.* Garden City, N.Y.: Doubleday, 1967.

Berger, Peter L., and Thomas Luckmann. *The Social Construction of Reality: A Treatise in the Sociology of Knowledge.* Anchor Books ed. Garden City, N.Y.: Doubleday, 1967.

Bevans, Stephen B. *Models of Contextual Theology.* Rev. and expanded ed. Faith and Cultures Series. Maryknoll, N.Y.: Orbis Books, 2002.

Bischoff, Claire, and Mary Elizabeth Mullino Moore. "Cultivating a Spirit for Justice and Peace: Teaching through Oral History." *Religious Education* (in press).

Blount, Brian K. *Cultural Interpretation: Reorienting New Testament Criticism.* Minneapolis: Fortress Press, 1995.

Bowers, C. A., and David J. Flinders. *Responsive Teaching: An Ecological Approach to Classroom Patterns of Language, Culture, and Thought.* Advances in Contemporary Educational Thought Series 4. New York: Teachers College Press, 1990.

Boyd, Robin H. S. *An Introduction to Indian Christian Theology.* Madras: Christian Literature Society, 1969.

Carroll, Jackson W., and Becky R. McMillan. *God's Potters: Pastoral Leadership and the Shaping of Congregations.* Grand Rapids, Mich.: William B. Eerdmans, 2006.

Chopp, Rebecca S. *The Power to Speak: Feminism, Language, God.* New York: Crossroad, 1989.

———. "When the Center Cannot Contain the Margins." In *The Education of the Practical Theologian,* ed. David Polk, Don Browning, and Ian Evison, 63–76. Atlanta: Scholars Press, 1989.

———. *Saving Work: Feminist Practices of Theological Education.* Louisville: Westminster John Knox Press, 1995.

Chua, How Chuang. "Hermeneutical Concerns in Contextualization." In *Trinity Evangelical Seminary Research Papers,* 2005.

Coe, Shoki. *Joint Action for Mission in Formosa.* Geneva: World Council of Churches, 1968.

———. "In Search of Renewal in Theological Education." *Theological Education* 9 (Summer 1973): 233–43.

———. "Contextualizing Theology." In *Mission Trends No. 3: Third World Theologies,* ed. Gerald H. Anderson and Thomas F. Stransky. New York: Paulist Press, 1976.

———. *Recollections and Reflections.* Ed. Boris Anderson, 2nd ed. New York: Coe Memorial Fund, 1993.

Cone, Cecil Wayne. *The Identity Crisis in Black Theology.* Nashville: AMEC, 1975.

Cone, James H. *A Black Theology of Liberation.* C. Eric Lincoln Series in Black Religion. Philadelphia: Lippincott, 1970.

———. "The Gospel and the Liberation of the Poor." *Christian Century* (1981): 162–66.

———. *Martin & Malcolm & America: A Dream or a Nightmare.* Maryknoll, N.Y.: Orbis Books, 1992.

———. *Risks of Faith: The Emergence of a Black Theology of Liberation, 1968–1998.* Boston: Beacon Press, 1999.

Daly, Mary. *Beyond God the Father: Toward a Philosophy of Women's Liberation.* Boston: Beacon Press, 1985.

Delamarter, Steve, Javier Alanís, Russell Haitch, Mark Vitalis Hoffman, Arun W. Jones, and Brent A. Strawn. "Technology, Pedagogy, and Transformation in Theological Education: Five Case Studies." *Teaching Theology and Religion* 10, no. 2 (April 2007): 64–79.

Dewey, John. *How We Think: A Restatement of the Relation of Reflective Thinking to the Educative Process.* Boston and New York: D. C. Heath, 1933.

Dobbs-Allsopp, F. W. *Lamentations.* Louisville: John Knox, 2002.

———. "The Delight of Beauty and Song of Songs 4:1–7." *Interpretation* 59 (2005): 260–77.

Dysinger, Luke. "Accepting the Embrace of God: The Ancient Art of Lectio Divina." *www.valyermo.com/ld-art.html.* Accessed May 16, 2007.

Farley, Edward. *Theologia: The Fragmentation and Unity of Theological Education.* Philadelphia: Fortress Press, 1983.

———. *The Fragility of Knowledge: Theological Education in the Church and the University.* Philadelphia: Fortress Press, 1988.

Fee, Gordon D. *New Testament Exegesis: A Handbook for Students and Pastors.* Rev. ed. Leominster, U.K., and Louisville: Gracewing and Westminster/John Knox Press, 1993.

Forche, Carolyn. *Against Forgetting: Twentieth Century Poetry of Witness.* New York: W. W. Norton, 1993.

Foster, Charles R., and Carnegie Foundation for the Advancement of Teaching. *Educating Clergy: Teaching Practices and the Pastoral Imagination.* San Francisco: Jossey-Bass, 2006.

Fox, Michael V. *The Song of Songs and the Ancient Egyptian Love Songs.* Madison: University of Wisconsin Press, 1985.

Gardner, Howard, Mihaly Csikszentmihalyi, and William Damon. *Good Work: When Excellence and Ethics Meet.* New York: Basic Books, 2001.

Geertz, Clifford. *Local Knowledge: Further Essays in Interpretive Anthropology.* New York: Basic Books, 2000.

Gilpin, W. Clark. *A Preface to Theology.* Chicago: University of Chicago Press, 1996.

Gorer, Geoffrey. *Death, Grief, and Mourning.* New York: Anchor Books Doubleday, 1967.

Grant, Jacquelyn. *White Women's Christ and Black Women's Jesus: Feminist Christology and Womanist Response.* American Academy of Religion Academy Series 64. Atlanta: Scholars Press, 1989.

Greene, Maxine. *Releasing the Imagination: Essays on Education, the Arts, and Social Change.* Jossey-Bass Education Series. San Francisco: Jossey-Bass Publishers, 2000.

Grey, Mary C. *Introducing Feminist Images of God.* Introductions in Feminist Theology 7. Sheffield: Sheffield Academic Press, 2001.

Griffiths, Paul J. "Reading as a Spiritual Discipline." In *The Scope of Our Art: The Vocation of the Theological Teacher,* ed. L. Gregory Jones and Stephanie Paulsell, 32–47. Grand Rapids: Eerdmans, 2002.

Gula, Richard M. *Moral Discernment.* New York: Paulist Press, 1997.

Hallo, W. W., and K. L. Younger, eds. *The Context of Scripture.* 3 vols. Leiden: Brill, 1997–2002.

Hampson, Margaret Daphne. *After Christianity.* London: SCM Press, 1996.

Hilfiker, David. *Urban Injustice: How Ghettos Happen.* New York: Seven Stories Press, 2003.

Holland, Joe, and Peter J. Henriot. *Social Analysis: Linking Faith and Justice.* Rev. and enl. ed. Maryknoll, N.Y.: Orbis Books, 1983.

hooks, bell. *Teaching to Transgress: Education as the Practice of Freedom.* New York: Routledge, 1994.

Hwang, C. H. *Joint Action for Mission in Formosa: A Call for Advance into a New Era.* Geneva: World Council of Churches, 1968.

Johnson, Elizabeth A. "To Let the Symbol Sing Again." *Theology Today* 51 (1997).

Johnson, Luke Timothy. *Decision Making in the Church: A Biblical Model.* Philadelphia: Fortress Press, 1983.

———. *The Writings of the New Testament: An Interpretation.* Philadelphia: Fortress Press, 1986.

———. *Faith's Freedom: A Classic Spirituality for Contemporary Christians.* Minneapolis: Fortress Press, 1990.

———. *The Real Jesus.* San Francisco: HarperSanFrancisco, 1996.

———. *Scripture and Discernment: Decision Making in the Church.* Nashville: Abingdon, 1996.

Johnson, Luke Timothy, and William S. Kurz. *The Future of Catholic Biblical Scholarship: A Constructive Conversation.* Grand Rapids: W. B. Eerdmans, 2002.

Johnson, Steven. *Everything Bad Is Good for You: How Today's Popular Culture Is Actually Making Us Smarter.* New York: Riverhead Books, 2005.

Johnston, Robert K. *Useless Beauty: Ecclesiastes through the Lens of Contemporary Film.* Grand Rapids: Baker Academic, 2004.

Jones, Serene. *Feminist Theory and Christian Theology: Cartographies of Grace.* Guides to Theological Inquiry. Minneapolis: Fortress Press, 2000.

———. "Graced Practices: Excellence and Freedom in the Christian Life." In *Practicing Theology: Beliefs and Practices in Christian Life,* ed. Dorothy C. Bass and Miroslav Volf, 51–77. Grand Rapids: Eerdmans, 2002.

Kawin, Bruce F. *Telling It Again and Again: Repetition in Literature and Film.* Ithaca, N.Y.: Cornell University Press, 1972.

Keel, Othmar. *The Song of Songs: A Continental Commentary.* 1st Fortress ed. Continental Commentaries. Minneapolis: Fortress Press, 1994.

Keillor, Garrison. *Good Poems.* New York: Viking, 2002.

Killen, Patricia O'Connell, and John De Beer. *The Art of Theological Reflection.* New York: Crossroad, 1994.

Kinast, Robert L. *Let Ministry Teach: A Guide to Theological Reflection.* Collegeville, Minn.: Liturgical Press, 1996.

King, Martin Luther, and James Melvin Washington. *A Testament of Hope: The Essential Writings of Martin Luther King, Jr.* San Francisco: Harper & Row, 1986.

Kinzie, Mary. *A Poet's Guide to Poetry.* Chicago Guides to Writing, Editing, and Publishing. Chicago: University of Chicago Press, 1999.

Lang, Berel, and Aron Appelfeld. *Writing and the Holocaust.* New York: Holmes & Meier, 1988.

Lawrence, D. H. *The Complete Poems of D. H. Lawrence.* Ed. Vivian de Sola Pinto and Warren Roberts. 2 vols. New York: Viking, 1964.

Linafelt, Tod. "Biblical Love Poetry (...And God)." *Journal of the American Academy of Religion* 70 (2002): 323–45.

Longenbach, James. *The Resistance to Poetry.* Chicago: University of Chicago Press, 2004.

Manguel, Alberto. *Into the Looking-Glass Wood: Essays on Books, Reading, and the World.* 1st Harvest ed. San Diego: Harcourt, 2000.

McDougall, Joy Ann. "Weaving Garments of Grace: En-gendering a Theology of the Call to Ordained Ministry for Women Today." *Theological Education* 39, no. 2 (2003): 149–63.

McKenzie, Steven L., and Stephen R. Haynes. *To Each Its Own Meaning: An Introduction to Biblical Criticisms and Their Application.* Rev. and expanded ed. Louisville: Westminster John Knox Press, 1999.

Moore, Mary Elizabeth. *Teaching from the Heart: Theology and Educational Method.* Harrisburg, Pa.: Trinity Press International, 1998.

———. *Teaching as a Sacramental Act.* Cleveland: Pilgrim Press, 2004.

Neruda, Pablo. *The Poetry of Pablo Neruda.* Ed. Ilan Stavans. New York: Farrar, Straus, Giroux, 2003.

Norris, Kathleen. *Amazing Grace: A Vocabulary of Faith.* New York: Riverhead Books, 1998.

Oden, Amy, ed. *In Her Words: Women's Writings in the History of Christian Thought.* Nashville: Abingdon, 1994.

Olds, Sharon. *The Gold Cell: Poems.* New York: Knopf, 1987.

Parini, Jay, ed. *The Wadsworth Anthology of Poetry.* Boston: Thomas Wadsworth, 2006.

Parratt, John. *An Introduction to Third World Theologies.* Cambridge and New York: Cambridge University Press, 2004.

Patton, John. *From Ministry to Theology: Pastoral Action and Reflection.* Nashville: Abingdon, 1990.

Plank, Karl A. "Ascent to Darker Hills: Psalm 121 and Its Poetic Revision." *Literature and Theology* 11 (1997): 152–67.

Roberts, J. Deotis. "Liberating Theological Education: Can Our Seminaries Be Saved?" *Christian Century* 100, no. 4 (1983): 113–16.

Roncace, Mark, and Patrick Gray, eds. *Teaching the Bible: Practical Strategies for Classroom Instruction.* Resources for Biblical Study 49. Atlanta: Society of Biblical Literature, 2005.

Roncace, Mark, and Patrick Gray, eds. *Teaching the Bible through Popular Culture.* Atlanta: Society of Biblical Literature, 2007.

Ruether, Rosemary Radford. *Women and Redemption: A Theological History.* Minneapolis: Fortress Press, 1998.

Scarry, Elaine. *On Beauty and Being Just.* Princeton, N.J.: Princeton University Press, 1999.

Schiff, Hilda. *Holocaust Poetry.* 1st U.S. ed. New York: St. Martin's Press, 1995.

Schneiders, Sandra Marie. *The Revelatory Text: Interpreting the New Testament as Sacred Scripture.* 2nd ed. Collegeville, Minn.: Liturgical Press, 1999.

Schön, Donald A. *Educating the Reflective Practitioner.* Jossey-Bass Higher Education Series. San Francisco: Jossey-Bass, 1987.

Schreiter, Robert J. *Constructing Local Theologies.* Maryknoll, N.Y.: Orbis Books, 1985.

———. *Faces of Jesus in Africa.* Maryknoll, N.Y.: Orbis Books, 1991.

———. *A New Catholicity: Theology between the Global and the Local.* Maryknoll, N.Y.: Orbis Books, 1997.

Shenk, Wilbert R. *Changing Frontiers of Mission.* Maryknoll, N.Y.: Orbis Books, 1999.

Shulman, Lee. "Teacher Development: Roles of Domain Experience and Pedagogical Knowledge." *Journal of Applied Developmental Psychology* 21, no. 1 (2000): 129–35.

Steiner, George. *Language and Silence: Essays on Language, Literature, and the Inhuman.* New York: Atheneum, 1967.

Sugirtharajah, R. S. *Asian Faces of Jesus.* Faith and Cultures Series. Maryknoll, N.Y.: Orbis Books, 1993.

Sullivan, William M. *Work and Integrity: The Crisis and Promise of Professionalism in America.* New York: HarperBusiness, 1995.

Szymborska, Wislawa. "Hunger Camp at Jaslo." In *Against Forgetting: Twentieth-Century Poetry of Witness,* ed. Carolyn Forche. New York: W. W. Norton, 1993), 459–60.

Tanner, Kathryn. "Social Theory Concerning the New Social Movements and the Practice of Feminist Theology." In *Horizons in Feminist Theology: Identity, Tradition, and Norms,* ed. Rebecca S. Chopp and Sheila Greeve Devaney, 179–97. Minneapolis: Fortress Press, 1997.

Thurman, Howard. *Jesus and the Disinherited.* Boston: Beacon Press, 1996.

Tiffany, Frederick C., and S. H. Ringe. *Biblical Interpretation: A Roadmap.* Nashville: Abingdon, 1996.

Vanhoozer, Kevin J., Charles A. Anderson, and Michael J. Sleasman, eds. *Everyday Theology: How to Read Cultural Texts and Interpret Trends.* Grand Rapids: Baker Academic, 2007.

Volf, Miroslav, and Dorothy C. Bass. *Practicing Theology: Beliefs and Practices in Christian Life.* Grand Rapids: W. B. Eerdmans, 2002.

Wenger, Etienne. *Communities of Practice: Learning, Meaning, and Identity.* Cambridge: Cambridge University Press, 1998.

Wheeler, Ray. "The Legacy of Shoki Coe." *International Bulletin of Missionary Research* 26, no. 2 (April 2002).

Whitehead, James D., and Evelyn Eaton Whitehead. *Method in Ministry: Theological Reflection and Christian Ministry.* New York: Seabury Press, 1980.

Wilmore, Gayraud S., and James H. Cone. *Black Theology: A Documentary History, 1966–1979.* Maryknoll, N.Y.: Orbis Books, 1979.

Wood, Charles Monroe. *Vision and Discernment: An Orientation in Theological Study.* Scholars Press Studies in Religious and Theological Scholarship. Decatur, Ga.: Scholars Press, 1985.

World Council of Churches., *Ministry in Context: The Third Mandate Programme of the Theological Education Fund.* Bromley, U.K.: TEF, 1972.

*xxxchurch.com,* accessed January 22, 2007.